style your own

Kids' Knits

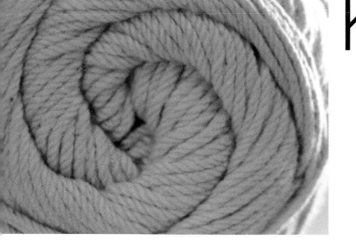

style your own
Kids' Knits

simply choose a pattern and
select a motif

Kate Buller

C&B

COLLINS & BROWN

I dedicate this book to Margery Dunstan

First published in Great Britain in 2002 by
Collins & Brown Limited
64 Brewery Road
London N7 9NT

A member of **Chrysalis** Books plc

Distributed in the United States and Canada
by Sterling Publishing Co,
387 Park Avenue South, New York, NY 10016, USA

2 3 4 5 6 7 8 9

British Library Cataloguing-in-Publication Data: A catalogue record
for this book is available from the British Library.

ISBN 1-85585-927-0

Conceived, edited and designed by Collins & Brown Ltd

PROJECT EDITOR: Clare Churly
ART EDITOR: Luise Roberts
MOTIF DESIGNER: Antonio Argenio
PATTERN EDITOR: Sharon Brant
PATTERN CHECKER: Eva Yates
COPY EDITOR: Eleanor Van Zandt
PHOTOGRAPHER: Colin Bowling
MODEL PHOTOGRAPHY: Danial Pangbourne

Acknowledgements
Thank you to Sharon Brant, Jane Crowfoot, Tracey Chapman, Heather Esswood, Mavis Hunt, Thelma Gardner, Helen Price for their countless hours of patient knitting.

Thank you to Polly Hardwicke, Jamie Yuill, Sam Morgan, Imogen Brook, Stevie Hope, Alexander Benson, Ethan O'Gorman, Millie Mulvaney, Francesca Sissons, George Gilham, Anthony Grant, Sophia Powell, Emily Sissons, Matthew Wadman, Joseph Rowe, Josephine Wadman and Kate Kingham for being the perfect models.

Thank you to Colin Bowling, Daniel Pangbourne and Eva Yates for their creative contributions.

Thank you to Rowan Yarns for supplying the yarn and all their support over the last 6 years.

Thank you to Kate Kirby for giving me the opportunity to do this book, Clare Churly for coordinating the project, Luise Roberts and Sharon Brant for their never ending enthusiasm and support, and last but not least to Antonio for the hundreds of motifs he designed and the many weekends he spent with me creating this book.

Reproduction by Global Colour Ltd, Malaysia

Printed and bound in Singapore by Imago

This book was typeset using Geometric and Goudy

Contents

Classic Garments 14
Before knitting **16**

Creative Library 78

Useful Techniques and Information 123

Introduction

Children's ever-changing sense of fashion and style makes most parents wonder how an earth they can keep up. From one day to the next its forever changing, governed as much by their mood when they wake in the morning as it is by what is hip, cool and 'lush' and being worn by all their friends and the latest teen band sensation.

That's why *Style Your Own Kids' Knits* may help, giving you lots of options and allowing you to stay one step ahead. Now pullovers, jackets, hats and bags can all celebrate your child's individuality by being customized according to their character and imagination. You can swap and change colours, and add style details and motifs as much as you like. Make your child feel that they are creating something new, which they can show off to their freinds, and that they are setting the fashion and not just following it.

I've tried to make this book as simple and easy to use as possible. Hopefully giving you both flexibility and all the tools you will need. If you've ever spent hours searching for a simple pattern for a classic V-neck pullover or jacket for a child, you'll welcome the collection in this book. What's more, you can have fun along the way by creating any number of permutations from the extensive library of designs and motifs. Never again can children say to you, that's boring, I don't like it. Now you'll always have an alternative up your sleeve.

Have Fun!

Kate Buller

How to use this book

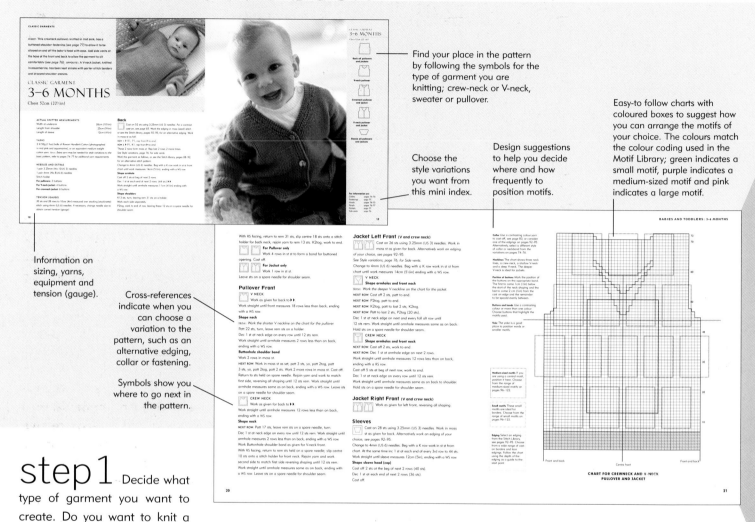

Find your place in the pattern by following the symbols for the type of garment you are knitting; crew-neck or V-neck, sweater or pullover.

Easy-to follow charts with coloured boxes to suggest how you can arrange the motifs of your choice. The colours match the colour coding used in the Motif Library; green indicates a small motif, purple indicates a medium-sized motif and pink indicates a large motif.

Choose the style variations you want from this mini index.

Design suggestions to help you decide where and how frequently to position motifs.

Information on sizing, yarns, equipment and tension (gauge).

Cross-references indicate when you can choose a variation to the pattern, such as an alternative edging, collar or fastening.

Symbols show you where to go next in the pattern.

step 1 Decide what
type of garment you want to create. Do you want to knit a jacket or a pullover, and would you prefer a round or a V-neck? You may know exactly what type of garment you want to knit, but why not also include the child in the decison?

step 2 Measure the child to help you decide which
size to knit. This book provides a separate pattern for eight different sizes, including babies, toddlers and children up to ten years old. However, children of the same age can differ in size so let the child's measurements, rather than his or her age, dictate which pattern to follow. Remember, it is far easier to alter the length of a garment than the width, so take this into account when you are selecting a pattern and choose the pattern that fits your child in width rather than length.

If you're not sure which pattern will fit your child, there is a 'magic' formula that you can use to help you decide which pattern is best.

Simply take two measurements: the circumference of the child's chest and the length of their arm from armpit to wrist. Then divide the chest measurment by four and add that number to the arm length. This is your child's 'magic' number. Do the same with the knitted measurments for each pattern, and choose a pattern whose 'magic' number is slightly larger than your child's. For example, if a three-year-old child has a chest measurement of 52cm (20½in) and an arm length of 21cm (8¼in), then their magic number would be 34cm (13½in). So, the best pattern for them would be the classic garment for 1–2 years which has a 'magic' number of 34.5cm (13½in).

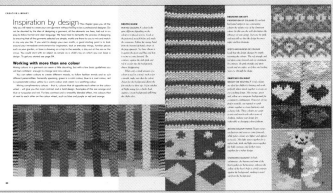

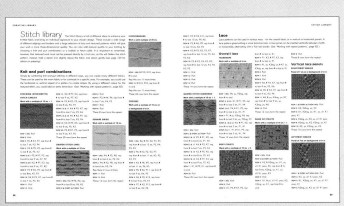

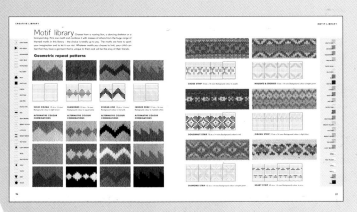

step 3

Once you have decided which type and size of garment you are knitting, you need to think about whether you want to knit the basic pattern or whether you want to vary the design. The four styles of each basic garment can be varied in many different ways. Choose from neckbands, collars, hoods, side vents, panels, fastenings, edgings and pockets. Instructions for these are given on in the section called **Style variations** (see pages 74–77).

step 4

You've chosen the design of the garment, now you need to personalize it. Think of it as a blank canvas. The section called **Inspiration by design** (see pages 80–87) helps you to make creative decisions about how to pick and mix colours and what textural effects go well together. Read this section before deciding what colour yarn to buy.

step 5

The basic patterns are given in moss stitch and stocking (stockinette) stitch. If you've decided to enhance your knitted fabric with alternative textures or edgings then turn to the **Stitch library** (see pages 88–95) for full pattern instructions. These include stitch patterns for different edgings and borders and a large selection of lace and textured patterns which will give your work a more three-dimensional quality. It also includes a selection of techniques for adding a textural quality to your knitting by choosing a knit and purl combination or a bobble or heart cable.

step 6

Finally, it is time to choose your motifs from the **Motif library** (see pages 96–122). Look through the themed motifs and select one or more that suits the garment and the child. There are three, colour-coded sizes of motif, small (green), medium (purple) and large (pink). The basic garment charts provide a guide to where the different sized motifs can be placed, but these are only suggestions; you can place your motifs wherever you like.

Yarns

Strands of spun fibre that have been twisted together to form a continuous thread are called yarn. It can be bought in different thicknesses and weights. Yarn manufacturers have created standard weight categories to make it easier to identify different weights of yarn. These vary slightly from one country to another. In the finer categories, the word 'ply' is often used (especially in Britain) to describe a yarn. The ply is the thread spun from fibres, and two, three or more plies may be twisted together to form the yarn. Generally, the lower the ply number, the thinner the yarn and the lighter the garment. However, the yarns available in each weight category are not necessarily identical, and the terms used simply indicate a similarity in tension (gauge) when knitted.

Yarns can be made from either natural or man-made fibres. Natural fibres include those of animal origin, such as wool, mohair, alpaca and silk, and those made from plant matter, such as cotton and linen. Man-made fibres include both regenerated natural fibres, such as viscose, and completly synthetic ones,

such as nylon and acrylic. Synthetic yarns are strong and hard-wearing but lack many of the finer qualities of natural-fibre yarns.

CHOOSING YARN

Cotton is a non-allergenic fibre with excellent absorbency and washing qualities, which make it excellent for children's knitwear. It is not itchy, is very soft on the skin and is suitable for wearing through most seasons

We have chosen to use Rowan Handknit Cotton for all of the garments in this book. This range has been chosen because of its wide spectrum of colours and because it has been specially treated to make it machine washable. The Handknit Cotton is a medium-weight 100% cotton yarn. It produces a clean crisp stitch, which makes it very suitable for multicolour knitting and shape definition.

SUBSTITUTING YARNS

When buying yarn it is always advisable to use the recommended brand. However if you are unable to obtain the yarn specified, use a similar weight of cotton or wool (*see page 126*). Try to buy as good-a-quality yarn as you can afford. After hours of knitting you could be very disappointed if you use a cheap substitute. The drape of the fabric may be limp and the wash properties poor, and the overall wearablity of the garment will be greatly reduced.

Fastenings
The way that you choose to fasten a garment can make a huge difference to the finished look. There are numerous fastenings you can choose, and they can be used in a decorative way to enhance the design and, of course, for practical purposes. For example, on the smaller-size pullovers I have added a button opening on the shoulder seam. This fastening will allow the garment to be put on and taken off the baby with ease.

Choose a large wooden button for an outdoor look; select a pretty mother-of-pearl button for a girl's pastel jacket intended for partywear. You can give a child's garment the most up-to-date fashion look by adding, say, a zip fastening to the front opening of the jacket or a small zip on a collar opening.

Think about the choice of fastening when purchasing the yarn for your garment. Most knitting stores and departments offer a wide range of buttons, zips, and poppers (snaps); or you could visit a specialist button shop for that extra-special touch. Secondhand shops are a wonderful source of unusual buttons. When selecting a zip it may not always be possible to find the exact size. This is not a problem; simply buy a longer size and cut it at the top to fit.

Lastly, always check that the buttons you choose are machine washable and non-toxic; this is especially important for babies' and toddlers' garments.

Equipment

To start knitting the projects in this book you will need only a few basic items. At the beginning of each pattern there is a list of equipment required. The most basic tool is the knitting needles. These can be made out of all sorts of materials including metal, plastic, bamboo and wood. The bamboo and wood needles are a little more expensive; however, many people prefer the way they feel in the hand.

Knitting needles come in a wide range of sizes and the pattern will specify the sizes recommended for that. However, you may need to use a different needle size to achieve the correct tension (gauge). Therefore it is a good idea to buy a size up and a size down as well as the size indicated. Avoid using needles that are damaged or have jagged ends, as they will slow down your knitting speed and may snag the yarn. All garments in this book need a stitch holder for holding the stitches on the neck shaping. If you are working motif designs on a garment you will also need bobbins to hold small amounts of yarn. Plastic bobbins are readily available from good yarn stores, or you can make your own from cardboard. Lastly, if you are adding a cable stitch or a cable edging to your garment, you will also need a cable needle.

Items that are not listed but are essential for all projects include the following: a tape measure, dressmakers' pins, scissors, a large tapestry or yarn needle with a blunt point for sewing up.

ESSENTIAL ITEMS

You will need the following for all the projects:

Tape measure A cloth tape to check your garment's measurements

Dressmakers' pins To pin out pieces of fabric for pressing or to join seams before sewing

Scissors A sharp pair of scissors to cut loose ends on knitting

Large tapestry or yarn needle A blunt-ended needle for sewing-up

NON-ESSENTIAL ITEMS

The following can be bought gradually:

Needle gauge To size unmarked, circular or double-pointed needles

Row counter To record the number of rows you have worked

Crochet hook To darn in ends at the back of the work or to pick up dropped stitches

Safety pins To hold a small number of stitches for a band or collar

Needle protector To prevent injury with the points of the needles

Knitting bag To keep your knitting clean and in one place

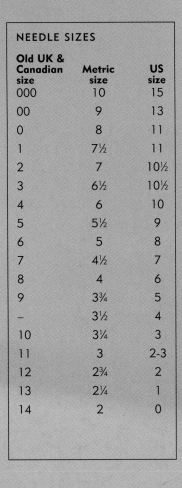

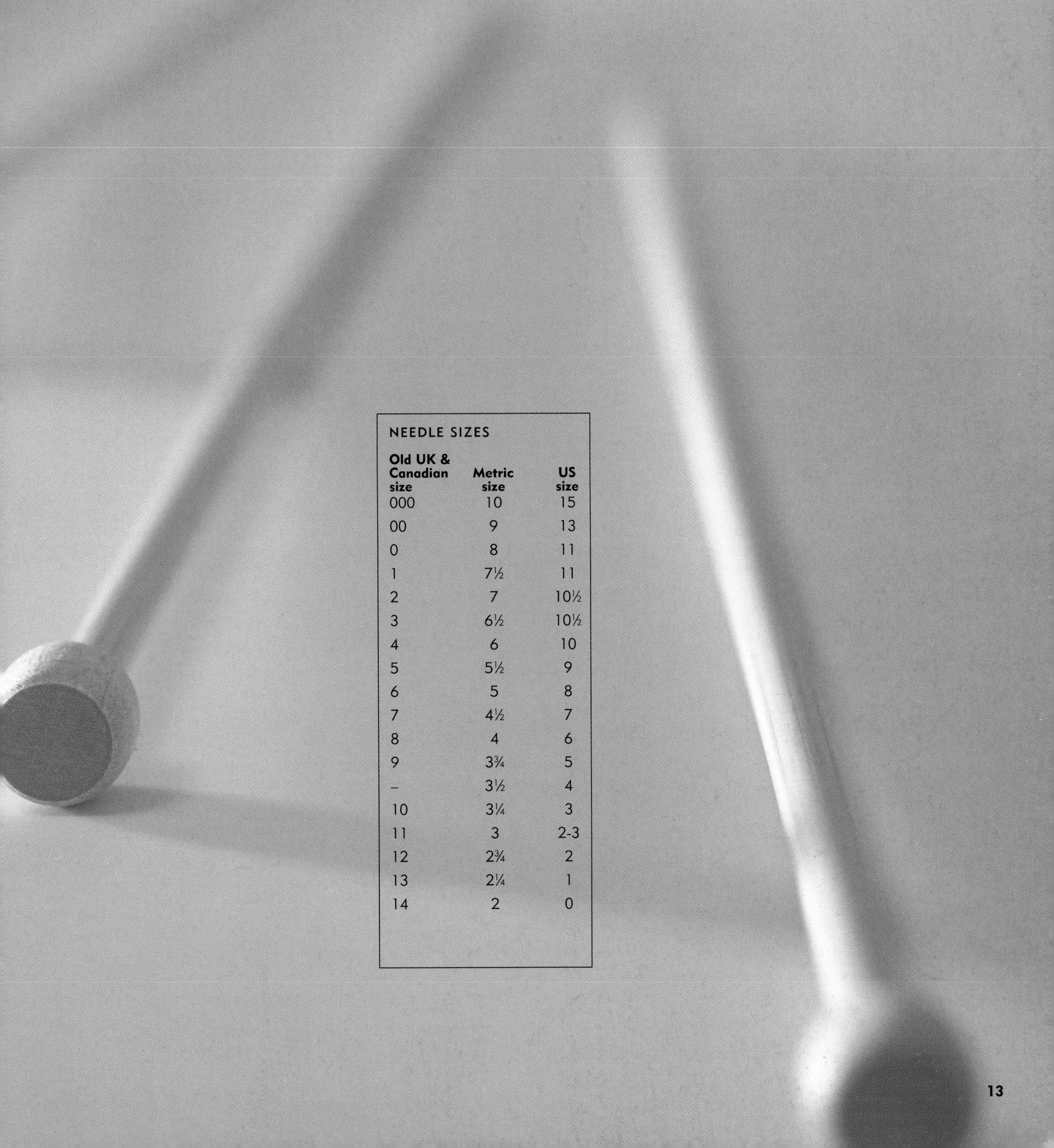

NEEDLE SIZES		
Old UK & Canadian size	**Metric size**	**US size**
000	10	15
00	9	13
0	8	11
1	7½	11
2	7	10½
3	6½	10½
4	6	10
5	5½	9
6	5	8
7	4½	7
8	4	6
9	3¾	5
–	3½	4
10	3¼	3
11	3	2-3
12	2¾	2
13	2¼	1
14	2	0

Classic garments

Older Children

Hats and bags

This chapter contains a basic wardrobe of classic children's garments, as well as some hats and bags. There are eight different garment sizes to include children up to ten years of age. Photographed on a mixture of boys and girls, they are all unisex. Your choice of colour, stitch pattern and finishing details will make the garment unique for your child. Each pattern is written to give you four styles of each basic garment. You can choose from either a round-neck or V-neck pullover or jacket. Each basic pattern is photographed showing two of the four styles, each with slightly different details, such as a decorative edging, or the addition of a collar or hood. These style variations can be added to any of the basic patterns, as described on pages 74–77.

Before knitting

In this book we have given you a separate pattern for eight different sizes, including babies, toddlers and children up to ten years old. Measure the child before choosing the size to knit. Each pattern gives you the actual size of the garment when finished. Children of the same age can differ in size, so you may find that the actual garment measurements for the pattern in your child's age range are not suitable for your child. If this is the case, then go with your child's measurements. Choose a different pattern or make some alterations to the pattern before you start knitting. It is far easier to alter the length of a garment than the width, so take this into account when you are selecting a pattern and choose the pattern that fits your child in width rather than length.

RECALCULATING MEASUREMENTS

First decide on the measurements required for a comfortable fit on your child. Then work out the difference between these measurements and the garment measurements given with the pattern. Using the stitch and row tension (gauge) of the pattern as a guide, first change the measurements into rows or stitches. Then follow the guidelines below.

HOW TO CHANGE SLEEVE LENGTH

This is done by altering the number of rows. The changes should be made after the cuff and before any shaping of the sleeve head (cap). Work the same number of stitch increases as given in the basic pattern, but recalculate to spread these increases across the new number of rows.

POCKET POSITIONING

Position pockets in the centre (horizontally) of the front sections.

HOW TO CHANGE THE WIDTH

To change the width of the garment, you need to alter the number of stitches per row. Once you have done this, however, you must remember to make corresponding changes to the number of stitches specified in the instructions for shaping the garment. Adjusting the width will also change the number of stitches you have for the shoulders and neck shaping.

ZIP FASTENING

Fasten the front opening with a zip to complete the fashion look.

CHECKING TENSION (GAUGE)

Tension (gauge) determines the size of the finished garment, so before starting, it is important to work a swatch to check that it matches the tension (gauge) stated in the pattern. Even a small difference can have an impact on the size of the garment.

To work a tension (gauge) square, cast on 30 stitches using 4mm (No.8/US 6) needles. Work the square over stocking (stockinette) stitch until the piece measures 14cm (5½in).

To count the stitches, measure 10cm (4in) horizontally across the square and mark this distance with pins. Count the number of stitches between the two pins, including any half-stitches.

To count the rows, repeat the same process vertically, this time counting the number of rows. It is easier to count the rows on the purl side of the work.

Adjust your tension (gauge) as follows: If you have too few stitches, your knitting is too loose and the garment will be too large; change to slightly smaller needles. If you have too many stitches, your knitting is too tight and the garment will be too small; change to slightly larger needles. If you do change the size of needles you use, you must also change the size of any other needles specified. It is more important to achieve the correct stitch tension (gauge) than the correct row tension (gauge).

HOOD
A hood can be added to the crewneck style to give a sporty look to a jacket.

HOW TO CHANGE THE LENGTH
To change the length of the garment, you need to alter the number of rows. Change the number of rows in the lower part of the garment, after the rib or border and before any armhole shaping.

RIGHT: This crewneck pullover, knitted in mid pink, has a buttoned shoulder fastening *(see page 77)* to allow it to be slipped on and off the baby's head with ease. Add side vents at the base of the front and back to allow the garment to sit comfortably *(see page 76)*. OPPOSITE: A V-neck jacket, knitted in aquamarine, has been kept simple with garter-stitch borders and dropped-shoulder sleeves.

CLASSIC GARMENT
3–6 MONTHS

Chest 52cm (20½in)

ACTUAL KNITTED MEASUREMENTS

Width at underarm	26cm (10¼in)
Length from shoulder	25cm (9¾in)
Length of sleeve	12cm (4¾in)

YARNS

3 X 50g (1¾oz) balls of Rowan Handknit Cotton (photographed in mid pink and aquamarine); or an equivalent medium-weight cotton yarn. **Note:** *Extra yarn may be needed for style variations to the basic pattern, refer to pages 74–77 for additional yarn requirements.*

NEEDLES AND EXTRAS

1 pair 3.25mm (No.10/US 3) needles
1 pair 4mm (No.8/US 6) needles
Stitch holder
For pullovers: 3 buttons
For V-neck jacket: 4 buttons
For crewneck jacket: 6 buttons

TENSION (GAUGE)

20 sts and 28 rows to 10cm (4in) measured over stocking (stockinette) stitch using 4mm (US 6) needles. If necessary, change needle size to obtain correct tension (gauge).

Back

 Cast on 52 sts using 3.25mm (US 3) needles. *For a contrast cast-on, see page 83. Work the edging in moss (seed) stitch or see the Stitch library, pages 92–95, for an alternative edging.* Work in moss st as foll:

ROW 1: ▶ K1, P1, rep from ▶ to end.
ROW 2: ▶ P1, K1, rep from ▶ to end.
These 2 rows form moss st. Rep last 2 rows 2 more times.
See Style variations, page 76, for side vents.
Work the garment as follows, or see the Stitch library, pages 88–92, for an alternative stitch pattern.
Change to 4mm (US 6) needles. Beg with a K row work in st st from chart until work measures 14cm (5½in), ending with a WS row.

Shape armhole
Cast off 2 sts at beg of next 2 rows.
Dec 1 st at each end of next 2 rows. (44 sts.) ▶ ▶
Work straight until armhole measures 11cm (4¼in) ending with a WS row.

Shape shoulders
K13 sts; turn, leaving rem 31 sts on a holder.
Work each side separately.
P2tog, work to end of row, leaving these 12 sts on a spare needle for shoulder seam

Chest 52cm (20½in)

**Back all pullovers
and jackets**

V-neck pullover

**Crewneck pullover
and jacket**

**V–neck pullover
and jacket**

**Sleeve all pullovers
and jackets**

For information on:

Collars	pages 74–76
Fastenings	page 77
Hoods	pages 74–75
Panels	pages 76–77
Pockets	page 77
Side vents	page 76

With RS facing, return to rem 31 sts, slip centre 18 sts onto a stitch holder for back neck, rejoin yarn to rem 13 sts. K2tog, work to end.

For Pullover only
Work 4 rows in st st to form a band for buttoned opening. Cast off.

For Jacket only
Work 1 row in st st.
Leave sts on a spare needle for shoulder seam.

Pullover Front

V NECK
Work as given for back to ▶ ▶.
Work straight until front measures 18 rows less than back, ending with a WS row.

Shape neck
Note: Work the shorter V neckline on the chart for the pullover.
Patt 22 sts, turn, leave rem sts on a holder.
Dec 1 st at neck edge on every row until 12 sts rem.
Work straight until armhole measures 2 rows less than on back, ending with a WS row.

Buttonhole shoulder band
Work 2 rows in moss st.
NEXT ROW: Work in moss st as set, patt 3 sts, yo, patt 2tog, patt 3 sts, yo, patt 2tog, patt 2 sts. Work 2 more rows in moss st. Cast off.
Return to sts held on spare needle. Rejoin yarn and work to match first side, reversing all shaping until 12 sts rem. Work straight until armhole measures same as on back, ending with a WS row. Leave sts on a spare needle for shoulder seam.

CREW NECK
Work as given for back to ▶ ▶.
Work straight until armhole measures 12 rows less than on back, ending with a WS row.

Shape neck
NEXT ROW: Patt 17 sts, leave rem sts on a spare needle, turn.
Dec 1 st at neck edge on every row until 12 sts rem. Work straight until armhole measures 2 rows less than on back, ending with a WS row.
Work Buttonhole shoulder band as given for V-neck front.
With RS facing, return to rem sts held on a spare needle; slip centre 10 sts onto a stitch holder for front neck. Rejoin yarn and work second side to match first side reversing shaping until 12 sts rem. Work straight until armhole measures same as on back, ending with a WS row. Leave sts on a spare needle for shoulder seam.

Jacket Left Front (V and crew neck)

Cast on 26 sts using 3.25mm (US 3) needles. Work in moss st as given for back. *Alternatively work an edging of your choice, see pages 92–95.*
See Style variations, page 76, for Side vents.
Change to 4mm (US 6) needles. Beg with a K row work in st st from chart until work measures 14cm (5½in) ending with a WS row.

V NECK
Shape armholes and front neck
Note: Work the deeper V neckline on the chart for the jacket.
NEXT ROW: Cast off 2 sts, patt to end.
NEXT ROW: P2tog, patt to end.
NEXT ROW: K2tog, patt to last 2 sts, K2tog.
NEXT ROW: Patt to last 2 sts, P2tog (20 sts).
Dec 1 st at neck edge on next and every foll alt row until 12 sts rem. Work straight until armhole measures same as on back. Hold sts on a spare needle for shoulder seam.

CREW NECK
Shape armholes and front neck
NEXT ROW: Cast off 2 sts, work to end.
NEXT ROW: Dec 1 st at armhole edge on next 2 rows.
Work straight until armhole measures 12 rows less than on back, ending with a RS row.
Cast off 5 sts at beg of next row, work to end.
Dec 1 st at neck edge on every row until 12 sts rem.
Work straight until armhole measures same as on back to shoulder.
Hold sts on a spare needle for shoulder seam.

Jacket Right Front (V and crew neck)

Work as given for left front, reversing all shaping.

Sleeves

Cast on 28 sts using 3.25mm (US 3) needles. Work in moss st as given for back. *Alternatively work an edging of your choice, see pages 92–95.*
Change to 4mm (US 6) needles. Beg with a K row work in st st from chart. At the same time inc 1 st at each end of every 3rd row to 44 sts.
Work straight until sleeve measures 12cm (5in), ending with a WS row.
Shape sleeve head (cap)
Cast off 2 sts at the beg of next 2 rows (40 sts).
Dec 1 st at each end of next 2 rows (36 sts).
Cast off.

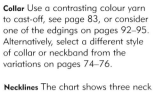

Collar Use a contrasting colour yarn to cast-off, see page 83, or consider one of the edgings on pages 92–95. Alternatively, select a different style of collar or neckband from the variations on pages 74–76.

Necklines The chart shows three neck lines, a crew-neck, a shallow V-neck and a deep V-neck. The deeper V-neck is ideal for jackets.

Position of buttons Mark the position of the buttons on the appropriate band. The first to come 1cm (½in) below the start of the neck shaping and the last to come 2 cm (¾in) from the cast on edge and the remainder to be spaced evenly between.

Buttons and bands Use a contrasting colour or more than one colour. Choose buttons that highlight the motifs used.

Yoke The yoke is a good place to position words or smaller motifs.

Medium-sized motifs If you are using a central motif, position it here. Choose from the range of medium-sized motifs on pages 96–122.

Small motifs These small motifs are ideal for borders. Choose from the range of small motifs on pages 96–122.

Edging Select an edging from the Stitch Library, see pages 92–95. Choose from a wide range of cast-on borders and lace edgings. Follow the chart using the depth of the edging as a guide to the start point.

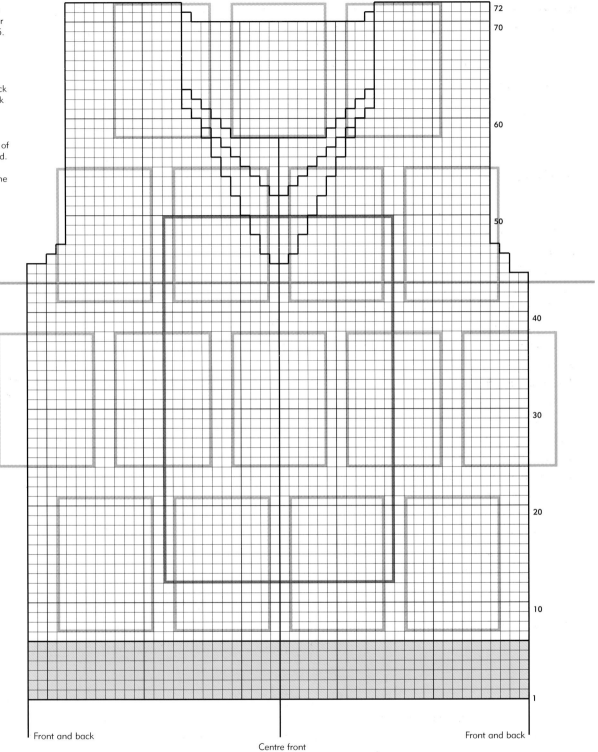

Front and back

Centre front

Front and back

CHART FOR CREWNECK AND V-NECK PULLOVER AND JACKET

21

SIMPLE FASTENINGS: *Use tiny shell buttons to finish off this simple baby's jacket. Alternatively, you could select a toggle or a larger button for a more outdoor look.*

buttonhole on row 3 as folls;

Patt to last 4 sts, patt 2 sts tog, yo, patt 2.

Work 3 more rows (6 rows in total). Cast off in patt.

CREW NECKBAND

With RS facing pick up and K 13 sts down left side of front neck, 10 sts from stitch holder, 13 sts up right side of front neck, 3 sts down right side of back neck, 18 sts from stitch holder and 3 sts up left side of back neck. (60 sts.)

Work the neckband as follows or choose an alternative neckband or collar, see Style variations, pages 74–76.

Work in moss st for 3 rows.

Place buttonhole as folls:

Patt 2 sts, yo, patt 2 sts tog, patt to end.

Work 2 more rows in moss st.

Cast off loosely and evenly in patt. *Alternatively work an edging of your choice; see pages 92–95.*

Finishing Jacket

Join both shoulders by knitting sts tog on the WS; *for casting (binding) off two edges together, see page 125.*

Finish the front bands or neckband as follows, or refer to Style variations, see pages 74–76, for an alternative neckband or collar.

V NECK FRONT BANDS

BUTTONHOLES: Make buttonholes on row 3. For a girl, on the right front band, patt 45 ▶ patt 2 sts tog, yo, patt 7 sts, rep from ▶ 2 more times, patt 2 sts tog, yo, patt 3. For a boy, on the left front band, patt 3 sts, ▶ yo, patt 2 sts tog, patt 7 sts, rep from ▶ 2 more times, yo, patt 2 sts tog, patt to end.

Right front band

With RS side facing, using 3.25mm (US 3) needles, beg at right front lower edge, pick up and K 35 sts up right front to beg of neck shaping, 30 sts up right side of neck, 3 sts down right side of back neck, 9 sts across to centre back of neck. (77 sts.)

For alternative fastenings and edgings, see Style variations, page 77.

Work in moss st for 6 rows. Cast off loosely and evenly in patt.

Alternatively work an edging of your choice, see pages 92–95.

Left front band

Work as given for Right front band, starting at Centre back neck.

For a contrast cast-off, see page 83.

Finishing Pullover

Join right shoulder by knitting sts tog on the WS; *for casting (binding) off two edges together, see page 125.*

V NECKBAND

With RS facing and using 3.25mm (US 3) needles, pick up and K 17 sts down left side of front neck, 1 st at centre of V and mark this st, 17 sts up right side of front neck, 3 sts down right side of back neck, 18 sts from stitch holder and 3 sts up left side of back neck. (59 sts.)

Work the neckband as follows or choose an alternative neckband or collar, see Style variations, pages 74–76.

Patt in K1, P1 rib, work to within 2 sts of marked st, work 2 sts tog, K centre marked st, work next 2 sts tog, patt to end.

Cont in rib as set, AT THE SAME TIME dec as set and place

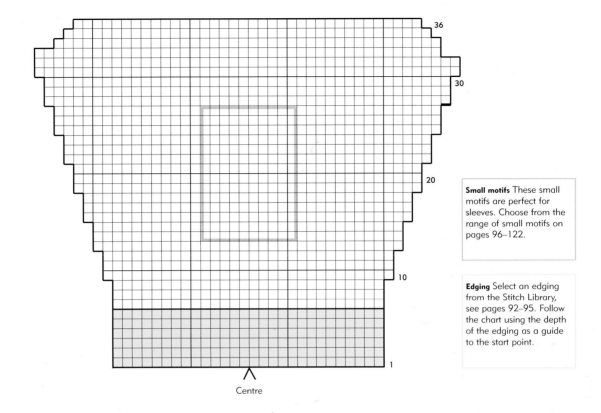

36

30

20

10

1

Centre

**CHART FOR SLEEVE FOR
PULLOVER AND JACKET**

Small motifs These small motifs are perfect for sleeves. Choose from the range of small motifs on pages 96–122.

Edging Select an edging from the Stitch Library, see pages 92–95. Follow the chart using the depth of the edging as a guide to the start point.

CREW NECK FRONT BANDS

BUTTONHOLES: Make buttonholes on row 3. For a girl on the right front band and for a boy on the left front band. Patt 3 sts, ▶ yo, patt 2 sts tog, patt 7 sts, rep from ▶ 3 more times, yo, patt 2 sts tog, patt 3.

Left front band

With RS facing and using 3.25mm (US 3) needles, pick up and K 44 sts along left front.

For alternative fastenings and edgings, see Style variations, page 77.
Work in moss st for 6 rows. Cast off loosely and evenly in patt.
Alternatively work an edging of your choice, see pages 92–95.

Right front band

Work as given for left front band.
For a contrast cast-off, see page 83.

Crew neckband

BUTTONHOLES: Depending on whether you are knitting for a boy or a girl, make a buttonhole on row 3 by either patt 2 sts, yo, patt 2 sts tog, patt to end, or patt to last 4 sts, patt 2 sts tog, yo, patt 2 sts.

Beg at front edge of right front band and using 3.25mm (US 3) needles pick up and K 6 sts across band, 18 sts up right side of neck, 3 sts down right back neck, 18 sts across back of neck, 3 sts up left back neck, 18 sts down left side of neck, 6 sts across left front band. (72 sts.) Work 6 rows in moss st.
Cast off loosely and evenly in patt. For a contrast cast-off, see page 83.
Alternatively work an edging of your choice; see pages 92–95.

Making Up

Press all pieces on WS with a warm iron over a damp cloth (or as instructions on yarn label), avoiding edging.
Join any alternative edging using a flat seam.
Using mattress stitch, sew in sleeves by joining cast-off sts at the beg of the armhole shaping to cast-off sts at start of sleeve-head shaping. Sew sleeve-head into armhole, easing in shaping.
Join side and sleeve seams.
Press seams.

RIGHT: A V-neck pullover worked as instructed in the master pattern – a classic shape for a baby. OPPOSITE: This crewneck jacket has been transformed into a pretty garment for a baby girl by adding a lacy edging to the lower edge (see pages 94–95) and a picot cast-off edge (see page 93) to the garter stitch collar (see page 75). The cuffs and front bands have also been worked in garter stitch (see page 93).

CLASSIC GARMENT
6–12 MONTHS

Chest 60cm (23½in)

ACTUAL KNITTED MEASUREMENTS

Width at underarm	30cm (11¾in)
Length from shoulder	30cm (11¾in)
Length of sleeve	16cm (6¼in)

YARNS

4 × 50g (1¾oz) balls of Rowan Handknit Cotton (photographed in pastel blue and pastel pink); or an equivalent medium-weight cotton yarn. **Note:** Extra yarn may be needed for style variations to the basic pattern, refer to pages 74–77 for additional yarn requirements.

NEEDLES AND EXTRAS

1 pair 3.25mm (No.10/US 3) needles
1 pair 4mm (No.8/US 6) needles
Stitch holder
For pullovers: 3 buttons
For V-neck jacket: 4 buttons
For crewneck jacket: 6 buttons

TENSION (GAUGE)

20 sts and 28 rows to 10cm (4in) measured over stocking (stockinette) stitch using 4mm (US 6) needles. If necessary, change needle size to obtain correct tension (gauge).

Back

Cast on 60 sts using 3.25mm (US 3) needles. *For a contrast cast-on, see page 83. Work the edging in moss (seed) stitch or see the Stitch library, pages 92–95, for an alternative edging. Work in moss st as foll:*
ROW 1: ▶ K1, P1, rep from ▶ to end.
ROW 2: ▶ P1, K1, rep from ▶ to end.
These 2 rows form moss st. Rep last 2 rows 2 times more.
See Style variations, page 76, for Side vents.
Work the garment as follows, or see the Stitch library, pages 88–92, for an alternative stitch pattern.
Change to 4mm (US 6) needles. Beg with a K row work in st st from chart until work measures 17.5cm (6¾in), ending with a WS row.
Shape armhole
Cast off 3 sts at beg of next 2 rows.
Dec 1 st at each end of next 3 rows (48 sts). ▶ ▶
Work straight until armhole measures 12.5cm (5in) ending with a WS row.
Shape shoulders
K14, turn, leaving rem 34 sts on a holder.
Work each side separately.
P2tog, work to end of row, leaving these 13 sts on a spare needle for shoulder seam.

**Back all pullovers
and jackets**

V-neck pullover

**Crewneck pullover
and jacket**

**V–neck pullover
and jacket**

**Sleeve all pullovers
and jackets**

For information on:

Collars	pages 74–76
Fastenings	page 77
Hoods	pages 74–75
Panels	pages 76–77
Pockets	page 77
Side vents	page 76

With RS facing, return to rem 34 sts, slip centre 20 sts onto a stitch holder for back neck, rejoin yarn to rem 14 sts. K2tog, work to end.

 For Pullover only

Work 4 rows in st st to form a band for buttoned opening. Cast off

For Jacket only

Work 1 row in st st.

Leave sts on a spare needle for shoulder seam.

Pullover Front

 V NECK

Work as given for back to ▶ ▶ .

Work straight until front measures 20 rows less than back, ending with a WS row.

Shape neck

Note: Work the shorter V neckline on the chart for the pullover.

Patt 24 sts, turn, leave rem sts on a holder.

Dec 1 st at neck edge on every row until 13 sts rem.

Work straight until armhole measures 2 rows less than on back, ending with a WS row.

Buttonhole shoulder band

Work 2 rows in moss st.

NEXT ROW: Work in moss st as set, patt 3 sts, yo, patt 2tog, patt 3 sts, yo, patt 2tog, patt 3 sts. Work 2 more rows in moss st. Cast off. Return to sts held on spare needle. Rejoin yarn and work to match first side, reversing all shaping until 13 sts rem. Work straight until armhole measures same as on back, ending with a WS row. Leave sts on a spare needle for shoulder seam.

CREW NECK

Work as given for back to ▶ ▶ .

Work straight until armhole measures 12 rows less than on back, ending with a WS row.

Shape neck

NEXT ROW: Patt 19 sts, leave rem sts on a spare needle, turn. Dec 1 st at neck edge on every row until 13 sts rem. Work straight until armhole measures 2 rows less than on back, ending with a WS row.

Work Buttonhole shoulder band as given for V-neck front.

With RS facing, return to rem sts held on a spare needle; slip centre 10 sts onto a stitch holder for front neck. Rejoin yarn and work second side to match first side reversing shaping until 13 sts rem. Work straight until armhole measures same as on back, ending with a WS row. Leaves sts on a spare needle for shoulder seam.

COMFORTABLE SHAPE: *A V-neck style sweater is ideal for babies as it allows that garment to be slipped on and off easily.*

Jacket Left Front (V and crew neck)

 Cast on 30 sts using 3.25mm (US 3) needles. Work in moss st as given for back. *Alternatively work an edging of your choice, see pages 92–95.*

See Style variations, page 96, for Side vents.

Change to 4mm (US 6) needles. Beg with a K row work in st st from chart until work measures 17.5cm (6¾in) ending with a WS row.

V NECK

Shape armholes and front neck

Note: Work the deeper V neckline on the chart for the jacket.

NEXT ROW: Cast off 3 sts, patt to last 2 sts, K2tog.

NEXT ROW: Patt to end.

NEXT ROW: K2tog at each end of row.

NEXT ROW: Work to last 2 sts; P2tog.

NEXT ROW: K2tog, patt to end (22 sts).

Dec 1 st at neck edge on next and every foll 3rd row until 13 sts rem. Work straight until armhole measures same as on back. Hold sts on a spare needle for shoulder seam.

CREW NECK

Shape armholes and front neck

Cast off 3 sts at beg of next row.

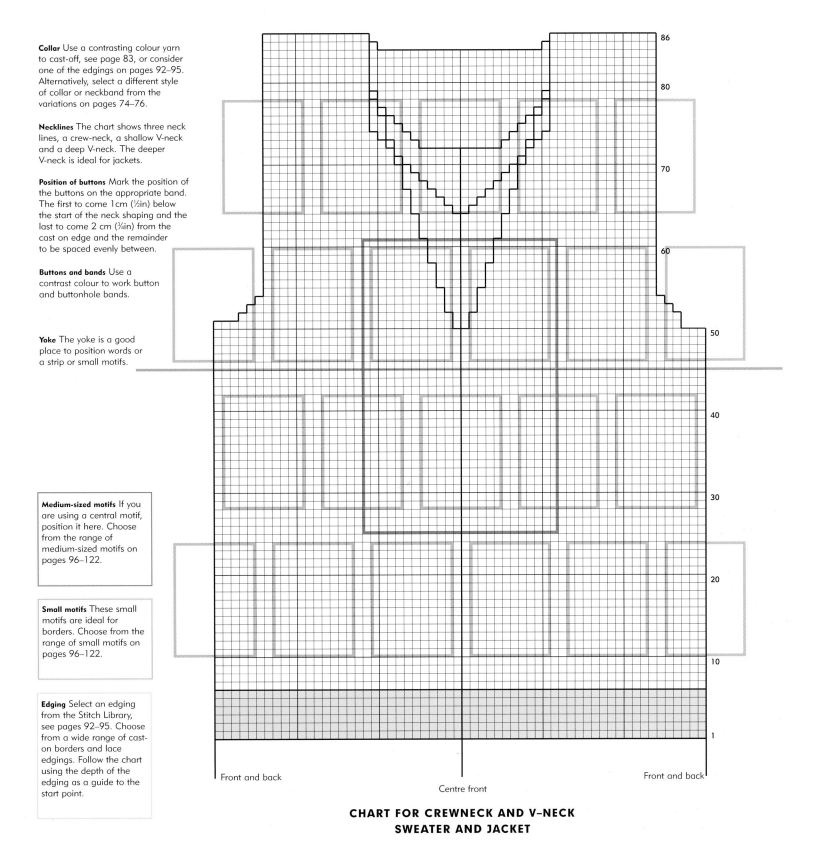

Collar Use a contrasting colour yarn to cast-off, see page 83, or consider one of the edgings on pages 92–95. Alternatively, select a different style of collar or neckband from the variations on pages 74–76.

Necklines The chart shows three neck lines, a crew-neck, a shallow V-neck and a deep V-neck. The deeper V-neck is ideal for jackets.

Position of buttons Mark the position of the buttons on the appropriate band. The first to come 1cm (½in) below the start of the neck shaping and the last to come 2 cm (¾in) from the cast on edge and the remainder to be spaced evenly between.

Buttons and bands Use a contrast colour to work button and buttonhole bands.

Yoke The yoke is a good place to position words or a strip or small motifs.

Medium-sized motifs If you are using a central motif, position it here. Choose from the range of medium-sized motifs on pages 96–122.

Small motifs These small motifs are ideal for borders. Choose from the range of small motifs on pages 96–122.

Edging Select an edging from the Stitch Library, see pages 92–95. Choose from a wide range of cast-on borders and lace edgings. Follow the chart using the depth of the edging as a guide to the start point.

Front and back

Centre front

Front and back

**CHART FOR CREWNECK AND V–NECK
SWEATER AND JACKET**

Dec 1 st at armhole edge on next 3 rows.

Work straight until armhole measures 12 rows less than on back, ending with a RS row.

Cast off 5 sts at beg of next row, work to end.

Dec 1 st at neck edge on every row until 13 sts rem.

Work straight until armhole measures same as on back to shoulder.

Hold sts on a spare needle for shoulder seam.

Jacket Right Front (V and crew neck)

 Work as given for left front, reversing all shaping.

Sleeves

 Cast on 32 sts using 3.25mm (US 3) needles. Work in moss st as given for back. *Alternatively work an edging of your choice, see pages 92–95.*

Change to 4mm (US 6) needles. Beg with a K row work in st st from chart. At the same time inc 1 st at each end of every 4th row to 50 sts. Work straight until sleeve measures 16cm (6¼in), ending with a WS row.

Shape sleeve head (cap)

Cast off 3 sts at the beg of next 2 rows (44 sts).

Dec 1 st at each end of next 3 rows (38 sts).

Work 1 row straight. Cast off.

Finishing Pullover

 Join right shoulder by knitting sts tog on the WS; *for casting (binding) off two edges together, see pages 125.*

V NECKBAND

With RS facing and using 3.25mm (US 3) needles, pick up and K 21 sts down left side of front neck, 1 st at centre of V and mark this st, 21 sts up right side of front neck, 3 sts down right side of back neck, 20 sts from stitch holder at back of neck and 3 sts up left side of back neck. (69 sts.)

Work the neckband as follows or choose an alternative neckband or collar, see Style variations, pages 74–76.

Patt in K1, P1 rib, work to within 2 sts of marked st, work 2 sts tog, K centre marked st, work next 2 sts tog, patt to end.

Cont in rib as set, AT THE SAME TIME dec as set and place buttonhole on row 3 as folls:

Patt 2 sts, yo, patt 2sts tog, patt to end.

Work 3 more rows in patt.

Cast off loosely and evenly in rib.

CREW NECKBAND

With RS facing pick up and K 15 sts down left side of front neck, 10 sts from stitch holder, 15 sts up right side of front neck, 3 sts down right side of back neck, 20 sts from stitch holder and 3 sts up left side of back neck. (66 sts.)

Work the neckband as follows or choose an alternative neckband or collar, see Style variations, pages 74–76.

Work in moss st for 3 rows.

Place buttonhole as folls:

Patt 2 sts, yo, patt 2 sts tog, patt to end.

Work a further 2 rows in moss st.

Cast off loosely and evenly in patt. *Alternatively work an edging of your choice; see pages 92–95.*

Finishing Jacket

Join both shoulders by knitting sts tog on the WS; *for casting (binding) off two edges together, see page 125.*

Finish the front bands or neckband as follows, or refer to Style variations, see pages 74–76, for an alternative neckband or collar.

V NECK FRONT BANDS

BUTTONHOLES: Make buttonholes on row 3. For a girl, on the right front band, patt 47 ▶ patt 2 sts tog, yo, patt 8 sts, rep from ▶ 3 more times, patt 2 sts tog, yo, patt 3. For a boy, on the left front band, patt 3 sts, ▶ yo, patt 2 sts tog, patt 8 sts, rep from ▶ 2 more times, yo, patt 2 sts tog, patt to end.

Right front band

With RS side facing, using 3.25mm (US 3) needles, beg at right front lower edge, pick up and K 38 sts up right front to beg of neck shaping, 32 sts up right side of neck, 3 sts down right side of back neck, 9 sts across to centre back of neck. (82 sts.)

For alternative fastenings and edgings, see Style variations, page 77.

Work in moss st for 6 rows. Cast off loosely and evenly in patt. Alternatively work an edging of your choice, see pages 92–95.

Left front band.

Work as given for Right front band, starting at Centre back neck.

For a contrast cast-off, see page 83.

CREW NECK FRONT BANDS

BUTTONHOLES: Make buttonholes on row 3. For a girl on the right front band and for a boy on the left front band. Patt 3 sts, ▶ yo, patt 2 sts tog, patt 10 sts, rep from ▶ 3 more times, yo, patt 2 sts tog, patt 3.

Left front band

With RS facing and using 3.25mm (US 3) needles, pick up and K 56 sts along left front.

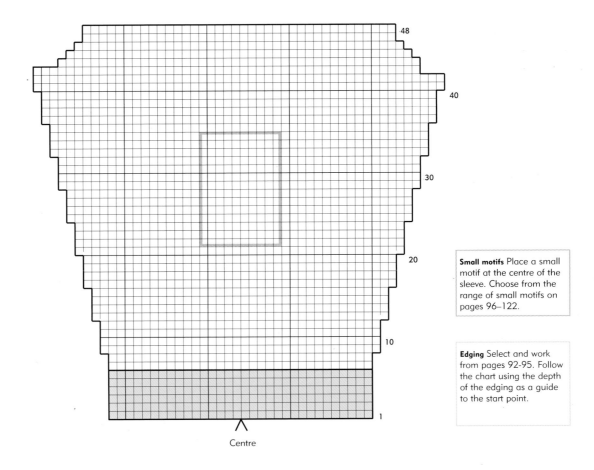

48

40

30

20

10

1

Small motifs Place a small motif at the centre of the sleeve. Choose from the range of small motifs on pages 96–122.

Edging Select and work from pages 92-95. Follow the chart using the depth of the edging as a guide to the start point.

∧
Centre

**CHART FOR SLEEVE FOR
PULLOVER AND JACKET**

For alternative fastenings and edgings, see Style variations, page 77.
Work in moss st for 6 rows. Cast off loosely and evenly in patt.
Alternatively work an edging of your choice, see pages 92–95.

Right front band
Work as given for left front band.
For a contrast cast-off, see page 83.

Crew neckband
BUTTONHOLES: Depending on whether you are knitting for a boy or a girl, make a buttonhole on row 3 by either patt 2 sts, yo, patt 2 sts tog, patt to end, or patt to last 4 sts, patt 2 sts tog, yo, patt 2 sts. Beg at front edge of right front band and using 3.25mm (US 3) needles pick up and K 6 sts across band, 18 sts up right side of neck, 3 sts down right back neck, 18 sts across back of neck, 3 sts up left back neck 18 sts down left side of neck, 6 sts across left front band. (72 sts.)
Work 6 rows in moss st.

Cast off loosely and evenly in patt. *For a contrast cast-off, see page 83. Alternatively work an edging of your choice; see pages 92–95.*

Making Up
Press all pieces on WS with a warm iron over a damp cloth (or as instructions on yarn label), avoiding edging.
Join any alternative edging using a flat seam.
Using mattress stitch, sew in sleeves by joining cast-off sts at the beg of the armhole shaping to cast-off sts at start of sleeve-head (cap) shaping. Sew sleeve-head (cap) into armhole, easing in shaping.
Join side and sleeve seams.
Press seams.

RIGHT: This V-neck jacket has K2, P2 ribbed borders *(see page 92)*. A small box collar *(see page 75)* has been added to the neck shaping. OPPOSITE: A ribbed shoulder detail has been added to this toddler's pullover *(see page 77)*. The edgings combine stocking (stockinette) stitch, which produces a rolled effect, with K2, P2 rib *(see page 93)*. Side vents complete the look *(see page 76)*.

CLASSIC GARMENT
1–2 YEARS

Chest 66cm (26in)

ACTUAL KNITTED MEASUREMENTS

Width at underarm	33cm (13in)
Length from shoulder	35cm (13¾in)
Length of sleeve	18cm (7in)

YARNS

5 × 50g (1¾oz) balls of Rowan Handknit Cotton (photographed in deep orange and mustard yellow); or an equivalent medium-weight cotton yarn. **Note:** *Extra yarn may be needed for style variations to the basic pattern, refer to pages 74–77 for additional yarn requirements.*

NEEDLES AND EXTRAS

1 pair 3.25mm (No.10/US 3) needles
1 pair 4mm (No.8/US 6) needles
Stitch holder
For V-neck jacket: 5 buttons
For crewneck jacket: 7 buttons

TENSION (GAUGE)

20 sts and 28 rows to 10cm (4in) measured over stocking (stockinette) stitch using 4mm (US 6) needles. If necessary, change needle size to obtain correct tension (gauge).

Back

Cast on 66 sts using 3.25mm (US 3) needles. *For a contrast cast-on, see page 83. Work the edging in moss (seed) stitch or see the Stitch library, pages 92–95, for an alternative edging.* Work in moss st as foll:
ROW 1: ▶ K1, P1, rep from ▶ to end.
ROW 2: ▶ P1, K1, rep from ▶ to end.
These 2 rows form moss st. Rep last 2 rows 2 times more.
See Style variations, page 76, for Side vents.
Work the garment as follows, or see the Stitch library, pages 88–92, for an alternative stitch pattern.
Change to 4mm (US 6) needles. Beg with a K row work in st st from chart until work measures 21cm (8¼in), ending with a WS row.
Shape armhole
Cast off 6 sts at beg of next 2 rows. ▶▶
Work straight until armhole measures 14cm (5½in) ending with a WS row.
Shape shoulders
K 17 sts; turn, leaving rem 37 sts on a holder.
Work each side separately.
P2tog, work to end of row, leaving these 16 sts on a spare needle for shoulder seam.
With RS facing, return to rem 37 sts, slip centre 20 sts onto a stitch

CLASSIC GARMENT
1–2 YEARS

Chest 66cm (26in)

**Back all pullovers
and jackets**

V-neck pullovers

**Crewneck pullover
and jacket**

**V–neck pullover
and jacket**

**Sleeve all pullovers
and jackets**

For information on:

Collars	pages 74–76
Fastenings	page 77
Hoods	pages 74–75
Panels	pages 76–77
Pockets	page 77
Side vents	page 76

holder for back neck, rejoin yarn to rem 17 sts. K2tog, work to end.
Work 1 row in st st .

Leave sts on a spare needle for shoulder seam.

Pullover Front

 V NECK

Work as given for back to .

Work straight until front measures 24 rows less than back, ending
with a WS row.

Shape neck

Note: Work the shorter V neckline on the chart for the pullover.

Patt 27 sts, turn, leave rem 27 sts on a holder.

Dec 1 st at neck edge on every row until 16 sts rem.

Work straight until armhole measures same as back, ending with a
WS row.

Leave sts on a spare needle for shoulder seam.

Return to sts held on spare needle. Rejoin yarn and work to match
first side, reversing all shaping until 16 sts rem. Work straight until
armhole measures same as on back, ending with a WS row. Leave sts
on a spare needle for shoulder seam.

ROLLNECK SWEATER: *A combination of a rib and stocking
(stockinette) stitch edging gives a trendy look to this toddlers sweater.*

 CREW NECK

Work as given for back to .

Work straight until armhole measures 16 rows less than on back,
ending with a WS row.

Shape neck

NEXT ROW: Patt 22 sts, leave rem 32 sts on a spare needle, turn.

Dec 1 st at neck edge on every row until 16 sts rem. Work straight
until armhole measures same as back, ending with a WS row. Leave
rem 16 sts on a spare needle for shoulder seam.

With RS facing, return to rem sts held on a spare needle; slip centre
10 sts onto a stitch holder for front neck. Rejoin yarn and work
second side to match first side reversing shaping. Leave rem 16 sts
on a spare needle for shoulder seam.

Jacket Left Front (V and crew neck)

 Cast on 33 sts using 3.25mm (US 3) needles. Work in
moss st as given for back. *Alternatively work an edging
of your choice, see pages 92–95.*

See Style variations, page 76, for Side vents.

Change to 4mm (US 6) needles. Beg with a K row work in st st from
chart until work measures 21cm (8¼in) ending with a WS row.

 V NECK

Shape armholes and front neck

Note: Work the deeper V neckline on the chart for the jacket.

NEXT ROW: Cast off 6 sts at beg of next row, work to last 2 sts, K2tog.
Work to end.

Dec 1 st at neck edge on next and every foll 3rd row until 16 sts
rem. Work straight until armhole measures same as on back. Hold
sts on a spare needle for shoulder seam.

 CREW NECK

Shape armholes and front neck

NEXT ROW: Cast off 6 sts at beg of next row.

Work straight until armhole measures 16 rows less than on back,
ending with a RS row.

Cast off 5 sts at beg of next row, work to end.

Dec 1 st at neck edge on every row until 16 sts rem.

Work straight until armhole measures same as on back to shoulder.
Hold sts on a spare needle for shoulder seam.

Jacket Right Front (V and crew neck)

  Work as given for left front, reversing all shaping.

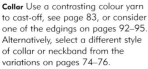

Collar Use a contrasting colour yarn to cast-off, see page 83, or consider one of the edgings on pages 92–95. Alternatively, select a different style of collar or neckband from the variations on pages 74–76.

Necklines The chart shows three neck lines, a crew-neck, a shallow V-neck and a deep V-neck. The deeper V-neck is ideal for jackets.

Position of buttons Mark the position of the buttons on the appropriate band. The first to come 1cm (½in) below the start of the neck shaping and the last to come 2 cm (¾in) from the cast on edge and the remainder to be spaced evenly between.

Buttons and bands Use a contrasting colour or more than one colour. Choose buttons that highlight the motifs used.

Yoke Consider introducing a change of colour or stitch detail at this point to create a yoke.

Medium-sized motifs If you are using a central motif, position it here. Choose from the range of medium-sized motifs on pages 96–122.

Small motifs These small motifs are ideal for borders. Choose from the range of small motifs on pages 96–122.

Edging Select an edging from the Stitch Library, see pages 92–95. Choose from a wide range of cast-on borders and lace edgings. Follow the chart using the depth of the edging as a guide to the start point.

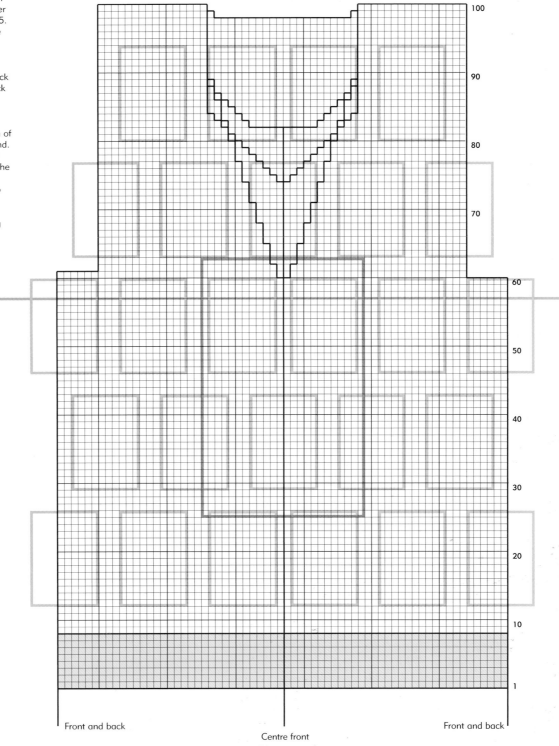

Front and back

Centre front

Front and back

CHART FOR CREWNECK AND V–NECK SWEATER AND JACKET

Sleeves

Cast on 32 sts using 3.25mm (US 3) needles. Work in moss st as given for back. *Alternatively work an edging of your choice, see pages 92–95.*

Change to 4mm (US 6) needles. Beg with a K row work in st st from chart. At the same time inc 1 st at each end of every 3rd row to 56 sts. Work straight until sleeve measures 18cm (7in), ending with a WS row.

Cast off.

Finishing Pullover

Join right shoulder by knitting sts tog on the WS; *for casting (binding) off two edges together, see page 125.*

V NECKBAND

With RS facing and using 3.25mm (US 3) needles, pick up and K 26 sts down left side of front neck, 1 st at centre of V and mark this st, 26 sts up right side of front neck, 4 sts down right side of back neck, 20 sts from stitch holder and 4 sts up left side of back neck. (81 sts.)

Work the neckband as follows or choose an alternative neckband or collar, see Style variations, pages 74–76.

Patt in K1, P1 rib, work to within 2 sts of marked st, work 2 sts tog, K centre marked st, work next 2 sts tog, patt to end.

Cont in rib as set, AT THE SAME TIME dec as set.

When rib measures 2cms (¾in).

Cast off loosely and evenly in rib.

Join shoulder seam and neckband.

CREW NECKBAND

With RS facing pick up and K 20 sts down left side of front neck, 10 sts from stitch holder, 20 sts up right side of front neck, 4 sts down right side of back neck, 20 sts from stitch holder and 4 sts up left side of back neck. (78sts.)

Work the neckband as follows or choose an alternative neckband or collar, see Style variations, pages 74–76.

Work in moss st for 2cms (¾in).

Cast off loosely and evenly in patt. Join shoulder seam and neckband.

Alternatively work an edging of your choice; see pages 92–95.

Finishing Jacket

Join both shoulders by knitting sts tog on the WS; *for casting (binding) off two edges together, see page 125.*

Finish the front bands or neckband as follows, or refer to Style variations, see pages 74–76, for an alternative neckband or collar.

STAND-UP COLLAR: *A shallow collar has been worked on this jacket which produces a collar that will stand up more. For a deeper collar that lies flatter, simply work more rows.*

V NECK FRONT BANDS

BUTTONHOLES: Make buttonholes on row 3. For a girl, on the right front band, patt 53 ▶ patt 2 sts tog, yo, patt 7 sts, rep from ▶ 3 more times, patt 2 sts tog, yo, patt 3. For a boy, on the left front band, patt 3 sts, ▶ yo, patt 2 sts tog, patt 7 sts, rep from ▶ 3 more times, yo, patt 2 sts tog, patt to end.

Right front band

With RS side facing, using 3.25mm (US 3) needles, beg at right front lower edge, pick up and K 44 sts up right front to beg of neck shaping, 36 sts up right side of neck, 4 sts down right side of back neck, 10 sts across to centre back of neck. (94 sts.)

For alternative fastenings and edgings, see Style variations, page 77.

Work in moss st for 6 rows. Cast off loosely and evenly in patt.

Alternatively work an edging of your choice, see pages 92–95.

Left front band

Work as given for Right front band, starting at Centre back neck.

For a contrast cast-off, see page 83.

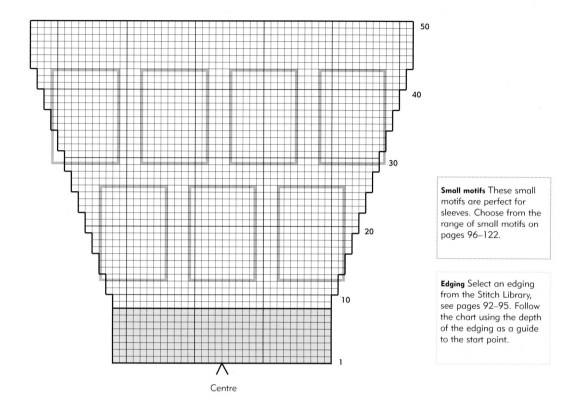

Centre

**CHART FOR SLEEVE FOR
PULLOVER AND JACKET**

Small motifs These small motifs are perfect for sleeves. Choose from the range of small motifs on pages 96–122.

Edging Select an edging from the Stitch Library, see pages 92–95. Follow the chart using the depth of the edging as a guide to the start point.

CREW NECK FRONT BANDS

BUTTONHOLES: Make buttonholes on row 3. For a girl on the right front band and for a boy on the left front band. Patt 2 sts, ▶ yo, patt 2 sts tog, patt 9 sts, rep from ▶ 4 more times, yo, patt 2 sts tog, patt 2.

Left front band

With RS facing and using 3.25mm (US 3) needles, pick up and K 61 sts along left front.

For alternative fastenings and edgings, see Style variations, page 77.
Work in moss st for 6 rows. Cast off loosely and evenly in patt.
Alternatively work an edging of your choice, see pages 92–95.

Right front band

Work as given for left front band.
For a contrast cast-off, see page 83.

Crew neckband

BUTTONHOLES: Depending on whether you are knitting for a boy or a girl, make a buttonhole on row 3 by either patt 2 sts, yo, patt 2 sts tog, patt to end, or patt to last 4 sts, patt 2 sts tog, yo, patt 2 sts.

Beg at front edge of right front band and using 3.25mm (US 3) needles pick up and K 6 sts across band, 25 sts up right side of neck, 4 sts down right back neck, 20 sts across back of neck, 4 sts up left back neck 25 sts down left side of neck, 6 sts across left front band. (90 sts.)
Work in moss st for 6 rows.
Cast off loosely and evenly in patt. *For a contrast cast-off, see page 83. Alternatively work an edging of your choice; see pages 92–95.*

Making Up

Press all pieces on WS with a warm iron over a damp cloth (or as instructions on yarn label), avoiding edging.
Join any alternative edging using a flat seam.
Using mattress stitch, sew in sleeves by joining cast-off sts at the beg of the armhole shaping to cast-off sts at start of sleeve-head shaping. Sew sleeve-head into armhole, easing in shaping.
Join side and sleeve seams.
Press seams.

RIGHT: A V-neck jacket with a sailor collar *(see page 75)*, worked in red, is a 'must' for any little boy's wardrobe.

OPPOSITE: A decorative cabled rib border *(see page 93)* enlivens the lower edge and sleeves, while a cabled high neckband *(see page 74)* has been added to the neck shaping for this pullover knitted in purple.

CLASSIC GARMENT
2–3 YEARS

Chest 74cm (29in)

ACTUAL KNITTED MEASUREMENTS

Width at underarm	37cm (14½in)
Length from shoulder	38cm (15in)
Length of sleeve	22cm (8¾in)

YARNS

7 × 50g (1¾oz) balls of Rowan Handknit Cotton (photographed in red and purple); or an equivalent medium-weight cotton yarn.

Note: *Extra yarn may be needed for style variations to the basic pattern, refer to pages 74–77 for additional yarn requirements.*

NEEDLES AND EXTRAS

1 pair 3.25mm (No.10/US 3) needles
1 pair 4mm (No.8/US 6) needles
Stitch holder
For V-neck jacket: 5 buttons
For crewneck jacket: 7 buttons

TENSION (GAUGE)

20 sts and 28 rows to 10cm (4in) measured over stocking (stockinette) stitch using 4mm (US 6) needles. If necessary, change needle size to obtain correct tension (gauge).

Back

Cast on 74 sts using 3.25mm (US 3) needles. *For a contrast cast-on, see page 83. Work the edging in moss (seed) stitch or see the Stitch library, pages 92–95, for an alternative edging. Work in moss st as foll:*

ROW 1: ▶ K1, P1, rep from ▶ to end.
ROW 2: ▶ P1, K1, rep from ▶ to end.
These 2 rows form moss st. Rep last 2 rows 3 times more
See Style variations, page 76, for Side vents.
Work the garment as follows, or see the Stitch library, pages 88–92, for an alternative stitch pattern.
Change to 4mm (US 6) needles. Beg with a K row work in st st from chart until work measures 37cm (14½in), ending with a RS row. ▶

Shape shoulders

P62, wrap foll st, turn the work. *For short-row shaping see page 124.*
NEXT ROW: K14, turn, leaving rem sts on a holder.
NEXT ROW: P2tog, work across all sts picking up loop of wrapped st.
Leave sts on a spare needle for shoulder seam.
With RS facing, return to rem 48 sts, slip centre 22 sts onto a stitch holder for back neck, rejoin yarn to rem 26 sts. K14, wrap foll st, turn the work. P12, P2tog, turn.
Work across all sts picking up loop of wrapped st.
Leave sts on a spare needle for shoulder seam.

2–3 YEARS

Chest 74cm (29in)

**Back all pullovers
and jackets**

V-neck pullover

**Crewneck pullover
and jacket**

**V–neck pullover
and jacket**

**Sleeve all pullovers
and jackets**

For information on:

Collars	pages 74–76
Fastenings	page 77
Hoods	pages 74–75
Panels	pages 76–77
Pockets	page 77
Side vents	page 76

Pullover Front

 V NECK

Work as given for back till work measures 23 rows less than the back, ending with a RS row.

Shape neck

Note: *Work the shorter V neckline on the chart for the pullover.*

Patt 37 sts, turn, leave rem sts on a holder.

Dec 1 st at neck edge on every row until 25 sts rem.

Work straight until work measures same as on back, ending with a WS row.

Shape shoulders

K13, wrap the next st, turn. *For short-row shaping see page 124.*

NEXT ROW: P13.

FOLL ROW: Work across all sts picking up loop of wrapped st.

Leave sts on a spare needle for shoulder seam.

Return to sts held on spare needle. Rejoin yarn and work 2nd side to match 1st side reversing all shaping.

 CREW NECK

Work as given for back, until work measures 15 rows less than on back, ending with a RS row.

Shape neck

NEXT ROW: Patt 30 sts, leave rem sts on a spare needle, turn.

Dec 1 st at neck edge on every row until 25 sts rem. Work straight until work measures same as the back, ending with a WS row.

NEXT ROW: K13, Wrap the next st, turn. *For short-row shaping see page 124.*

NEXT ROW: P13.

NEXT ROW: Work across all sts picking up loop of wrapped st.

Leave sts on a spare needle.

Return to sts held on a spare needle. Slip centre 14 sts onto a spare needle.

Rejoin yarn to rem 30 sts and work 2nd side to match 1st side reversing all shaping.

Jacket Left Front (V neck and crew neck)

 Cast on 37 sts using 3.25mm (US 3) needles. Work in moss st as given for back. *Alternatively work an edging of your choice, see pages 92–95.*

See Style variations, page 76, for Side vents.

Change to 4mm (US 6) needles. Beg with a K row work in st st from chart.

V NECK

Work until front measures 22cm (8½in) ending with a RS row

Shape front neck

Note: *Work the deeper V neckline on the chart for the jacket.*

NEXT ROW: Dec 1 st at beg of next row, work to end. Work 1 row.

Dec 1 st at neck edge on next and every foll 3rd row until 25 sts rem.

Work straight until work measures same as the back, ending with a RS row.

NEXT ROW: P13, wrap the next st, turn. *For short-row shaping see page 124.*

NEXT ROW: K13.

NEXT ROW: Work across all sts picking up loop of wrapped st.

Leave sts on a spare needle for shoulder seam.

 CREW NECK

Work until front measures 15 rows less than the back, ending with a RS row.

Shape front neck

NEXT ROW: Cast off 7 sts, work to end

Dec 1 st at neck edge on every row until 25 sts rem ending on a RS row.

Work straight until work measures same as back to shoulder, ending with a RS row.

NEXT ROW: P13, wrap the next st, turn. *For short-row shaping see page 124.*

NEXT ROW: K13.

NEXT ROW: Work across all sts picking up loop of wrapped st. Hold sts on a spare needle for shoulder seam.

Jacket Right Front (V and crew neck)

 Work as given for left front, reversing all shaping.

Sleeves

 Cast on 36 sts using 3.25mm (US 3) needles. *Work in moss st as given for back. Alternatively work an edging of your choice, see pages 92–95.*

Change to 4mm (US 6) needles. Beg with a K row work in st st from chart. At the same time inc 1 st at each end of every 4th row to 60 sts. Work straight until sleeve measures 23cm (9in), ending with a WS row.

Cast off.

Finishing Pullover

Join right shoulder by knitting sts tog on the WS; *for casting (binding) off two edges together, see page 125.*

Short-row shaping The orange highlighted row indicates the last row of short-row shaping, which is worked in order to hide the loop around the slipped stitch.

Collar Use a contrasting colour yarn to cast-off, see page 83, or consider one of the edgings on pages 92–95. Alternatively, select a different style of collar or neckband from the variations on pages 74–76.

Necklines The chart shows three neck lines, a crew-neck, a shallow V-neck and a deep V-neck. The deeper V-neck is ideal for jackets.

Position of buttons Mark the position of the buttons on the appropriate band. The first to come 1cm (½in) below the start of the neck shaping and the last to come 2 cm (¾in) from the cast on edge and the remainder to be spaced evenly between.

Buttons and bands Use a contrasting colour to cast off the bands to frame the front opening.

Yoke Consider introducing a change of colour or stitch detail at this point to create a yoke.

Central image If you are using a central motif, position it here. Choose from the range of large motifs on pages 96–122.

Medium-sized motifs These motifs can be effective when arranged in a pattern. Choose from the range of medium-sized motifs on pages 96–122.

Small motifs These small motifs are ideal for borders. Choose from the range of small motifs on pages 96–122.

Edging Select an edging from the Stitch Library, see pages 92–95. Choose from a wide range of cast-on borders and lace edgings. Follow the chart using the depth of the edging as a guide to the start point.

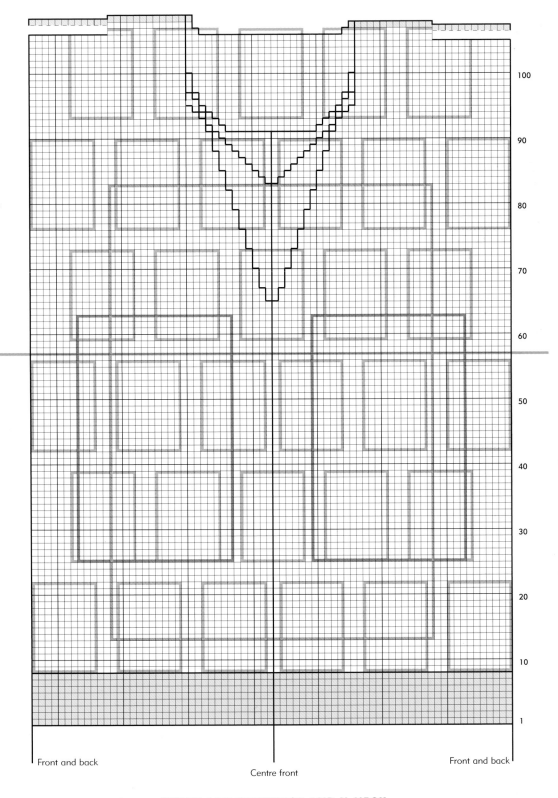

Front and back   Centre front   Front and back

**CHART FOR CREWNECK AND V-NECK
PULLOVER AND JACKET**

V NECKBAND

With RS facing and using 3.25mm (US 3) needles, pick up and K 28 sts down left side of front neck, 1 st at centre of V and mark this st, 28 sts up right side of front neck, 6 sts down right side of back neck, 22 sts from stitch holder at back of neck, 4 sts up left side of back neck (87 sts).

Work the neckband as follows or choose an alternative neckband or collar, see Style variations, pages 74–76.

Patt in rib st, work to within 2 sts of marked st, work 2 sts tog, K centre marked st, work next 2 sts tog, patt to end.

CABLED HIGH NECKBAND: *This high neckband and edging can be knitted to a deep or shallower depth, depending on the look that you wish to create.*

Cont in moss st as set, AT THE SAME TIME dec as set until band measures 2cm (¾in). Join left shoulder seam and neckband. Cast off loosely and evenly in patt.

CREW NECKBAND

With RS facing pick up and K 18 sts down left side of front neck, 14 sts from stitch holder at front of neck, 18 sts up left side of front neck, and 4 sts down left side of back neck, 22 sts from stitch holder at back of neck, 4 sts up right side of back neck. (80 sts.)

Work the neckband as follows or choose an alternative neckband or collar, see Style variations, pages 74–76.

Work in moss st for 2cm (¾in), then cast off loosely and evenly in patt. Join left shoulder seam and neckband. *Alternatively work an edging of your choice; see pages 92–95.*

Finishing Jacket

Join both shoulders by knitting sts tog on the WS; *for casting (binding) off two edges together, see page 125.*

Finish the front bands or neckband as follows, or refer to Style variations, see pages 74–76, for an alternative neckband or collar.

V NECK FRONT BANDS

BUTTONHOLES: Make buttonholes on row 5. For a girl, on the right front band, patt 55 ▶ patt 2 sts tog, yo, patt 8 sts, rep from ▶ 3 more times, patt 2 sts tog, yo, patt 3. For a boy, on the left front band, patt 3 sts, ▶ yo, patt 2 sts tog, patt 8 sts, rep from ▶ 3 more times, yo, patt 2 sts tog, patt to end.

Right front band

With RS side facing, using 3.25mm (US 3) needles, beg at right front lower edge, pick up and K 48 sts up right front to beg of neck shaping, 37 sts up right side of neck, 4 sts down right side of back neck, 11 sts across to centre back of neck. (100 sts.)

For alternative fastenings and edgings, see Style variations, page 77. Work in moss st for 8 rows. Cast off loosely and evenly in patt. *Alternatively work an edging of your choice, see pages 92–95.*

Left front band

Work as given for Right front band, starting at Centre back neck. *For a contrast cast-off, see page 83.*

CREW NECK FRONT BANDS

BUTTONHOLES: Make buttonholes on row 5. For a girl on the right front band and for a boy on the left front band. Patt 3 sts, ▶ yo, patt 2 sts tog, patt 12 sts, rep from ▶ 4 more times, yo, patt 2 sts tog, patt 3.

Left front band

With RS facing and using 3.25mm (US 3) needles, pick up and K 66 sts along left front.

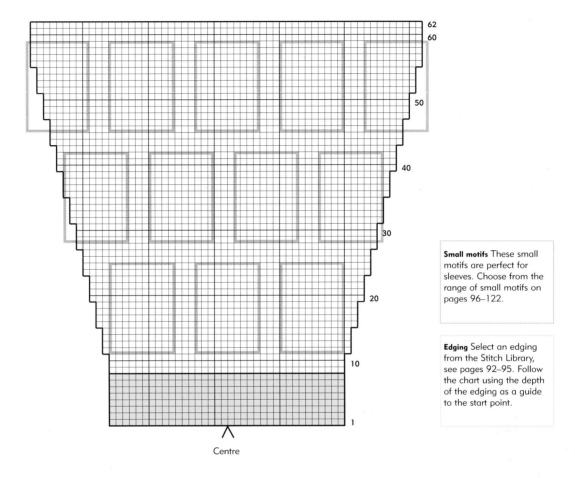

62
60

50

40

30

20

10

1

Centre

Small motifs These small motifs are perfect for sleeves. Choose from the range of small motifs on pages 96–122.

Edging Select an edging from the Stitch Library, see pages 92–95. Follow the chart using the depth of the edging as a guide to the start point.

CHART FOR SLEEVE FOR SWEATER AND JACKET

For alternative fastenings and edgings, see Style variations, page 77.
Work in moss st for 8 rows. Cast off loosely and evenly in patt.
Alternatively work an edging of your choice, see pages 92–95.

Right front band
Work as given for left front band.
For a contrast cast-off, see page 83.

Crew neckband
BUTTONHOLES: Depending on whether you are knitting for a boy or a girl, make a buttonhole on row 5 by either patt 2 sts, yo, patt 2 sts tog, patt to end, or patt to last 4 sts, patt 2 sts tog, yo, patt 2 sts.
Beg at front edge of right front band and using 3.25mm (US 3) needles pick up and K 8 sts across band, 24 sts up right side of neck, 4 sts down right back neck, 22 sts across back of neck, 4 sts up left back neck 24 sts down left side of neck, 8 sts across left front band. (94 sts.)

Work in moss st for 8 rows.
Cast off loosely and evenly in patt. *For a contrast cast-off, see page 83. Alternatively work an edging of your choice; see pages 92–95.*

Making Up

Press all pieces on WS with a warm iron over a damp cloth (or as instructions on yarn label), avoiding edging.
Join any alternative edging using a flat seam.
Using mattress stitch, sew in sleeves placing centre of cast off edge of sleeve to shoulder seam.
Join side and sleeve seams.
Press seams.

RIGHT: This crewneck jacket has a zip fastening *(see page 74)* and a hood for the most up-to-date fashion look. Pockets have also been added to the fronts *(see page 77).* OPPOSITE: A V-neck pullover kept simple with a cowl neck detail *(see page 74).* This style is easy to wear and suitable for any occasion.

CLASSIC GARMENT
4–5 YEARS

Chest 80cm (31½in)

ACTUAL KNITTED MEASUREMENTS

Width at underarm	40cm (15¾in)
Length from shoulder	42cm (16½in)
Length of sleeve	25cm (9¾in)

YARNS

8 X 50g (1¾oz) balls of Rowan Handknit Cotton (photographed in bright green and blue); or an equivalent medium-weight cotton yarn.
Note: Extra yarn may be needed for style variations to the basic pattern, refer to pages 74–77 for additional yarn requirements.

NEEDLES AND EXTRAS

1 pair 3.25mm (No.10/US 3) needles
1 pair 4mm (No.8/US 6) needles
Stitch holder
For V-neck jacket: 5 buttons
For crewneck jacket: 7 buttons

TENSION (GAUGE)

20 sts and 28 rows to 10cm (4in) measured over stocking (stockinette) stitch using 4mm (US 6) needles. If necessary, change needle size to obtain correct tension (gauge).

Back

Cast on 80 sts using 3.25mm (US 3) needles. *For a contrast cast-on, see page 83. Work the edging in moss (seed) stitch or see the Stitch library, pages 92–95, for an alternative edging.* Work in moss st as foll:
ROW 1: ▶ K1, P1, rep from ▶ to end.
ROW 2: ▶ P1, K1, rep from ▶ to end.
These 2 rows form moss st. Rep last 2 rows 3 times more
See Style variations, page 76, for Side vents.
Work the garment as follows, or see the Stitch library, pages 88–92, for an alternative stitch pattern.
Change to 4mm (US 6) needles. Beg with a K row work in st st from chart until work measures 40cm (15¾in), ending with a RS row. ▶
Shape shoulders
P72, wrap foll st, turn the work. *For short-row shaping see page 124.*
NEXT ROW: K20, turn, leaving rem sts on a holder.
NEXT ROW: P2tog, P9, wrap foll st. turn the work.
NEXT ROW: K8, K2tog.
NEXT ROW: Work across all sts picking up loops of wrapped sts.
Leave sts on a spare needle for shoulder seam.
With RS facing, return to rem 52 sts, slip centre 24 sts onto a stitch holder for back neck, rejoin yarn to rem 28 sts.
K20, wrap foll st, turn the work.

Chest 80cm (31½in)

**Back all pullovers
and jackets**

V-neck pullovers

**Crewneck pullover
and jacket**

**V–neck pullover
and jacket**

**Sleeve all pullovers
and jackets**

For information on:

Collars	pages 74–76
Fastenings	page 77
Hoods	pages 74–75
Panels	pages 76–77
Pockets	page 77
Side vents	page 76

NEXT ROW: P18, P2tog.

NEXT ROW: K2tog, K8, wrap foll st. Turn the work.

NEXT ROW: P8.

Work across all sts picking up loops of wrapped sts.

Leave sts on a spare needle for shoulder seam.

Pullover Front

 V NECK

Work as given for back till work measures 24 rows less than the back, ending with a WS row.

Shape neck

Note: Work the shorter V neckline on the chart for the pullover.

Patt 40 sts, turn, leave rem sts on a holder.

Dec 1 st at neck edge on every row until 26 sts rem.

Work straight until work measures same as on back, ending with a RS row.

Shape shoulders

P18, wrap the next st, turn. *For short-row shaping see page 124.*

NEXT ROW: K18.

NEXT ROW: P9, wrap the next st, turn.

NEXT ROW: K9.

FOLL ROW: Work across all sts picking up loop of wrapped st.

Leave sts on a spare needle for shoulder seam.

Return to sts held on spare needle. Rejoin yarn and work 2nd side to match 1st side reversing all shaping.

CREW NECK

Work as given for back, until work measures 16 rows less than on back, ending with a WS row.

Shape neck

NEXT ROW: Patt 33 sts, leave rem sts on a spare needle, turn.

Dec 1 st at neck edge on every row until 26 sts rem. Work straight until work measures same as the back, ending with a RS row.

Shape shoulders

P18, wrap the next st, turn. *For short-row shaping see page 124.*

NEXT ROW: K18.

NEXT ROW: P9, wrap the next st, turn.

NEXT ROW: K9.

FOLL ROW: Work across all sts picking up loop of wrapped st.

Leave sts on a spare needle.

Return to sts held on a spare needle. Slip centre 14 sts onto a spare needle.

Rejoin yarn to rem 33 sts and work 2nd side to match 1st side reversing all shaping.

Jacket Left Front (V and crew neck)

 Cast on 40 sts using 3.25mm (US 3) needles. Work in moss st as given for back. *Alternatively work an edging of your choice, see pages 92–95.*

See Style variations, page 76, for Side vents.

Change to 4mm (US 6) needles. Beg with a K row work in st st from chart.

 V NECK

Shape front neck

Note: Work the deeper V neckline on the chart for the jacket.

Work until front measures 26cm (10¼in) ending with a RS row.

NEXT ROW: Dec 1 st at beg of next row, work to end. Work 1 row.

Dec 1 st at neck edge on next and every foll 3rd row until 26 sts rem.

Work straight until work measures same as the back, ending with a RS row.

Shape shoulders

P18, wrap the next st, turn. *For short-row shaping see page 124.*

NEXT ROW: K18.

NEXT ROW: P9, wrap the next st, turn.

NEXT ROW: K9.

FOLL ROW: Work across all sts picking up loop of wrapped st.

Leave sts on a spare needle for shoulder seam.

 CREW NECK

Work until front measures 16 rows less than on back, ending with a RS row.

Shape front neck

NEXT ROW: Cast off 7sts, work to end

Dec 1 st at neck edge on every row until 26 sts rem ending on a RS row.

Work straight until work measures same as back to shoulder, ending with a RS row.

Shape shoulders

P18, wrap the next st, turn. *For short-row shaping see page 124.*

NEXT ROW: K18.

NEXT ROW: P9, wrap the next st, turn.

NEXT ROW: K9.

FOLL ROW: Work across all sts picking up loop of wrapped st.

Leave sts on a spare needle for shoulder seam.

Jacket Right Front (V and crew neck)

 Work as given for left front, reversing all shaping.

Short-row shaping The orange highlighted row indicates the last row of short-row shaping, which is worked in order to hide the loop around the slipped stitch.

Collar Use a contrasting colour yarn to cast-off, see page 83, or consider one of the edgings on pages 92–95. Alternatively, select a different style of collar or neckband from the variations on pages 74–76.

Necklines The chart shows three neck lines, a crew-neck, a shallow V-neck and a deep V-neck. The deeper V-neck is ideal for jackets.

Position of buttons Mark the position of the buttons on the appropriate band. The first to come 1cm (½in) below the start of the neck shaping and the last to come 2 cm (¾in) from the cast on edge and the remainder to be spaced evenly between.

Yoke Consider introducing a change of colour or stitch detail at this point to create a yoke.

Buttons and bands Use a contrasting colour to cast off the bands to frame the front opening. Choose buttons that enhance the motifs used.

Central image If you are using a central motif, position it here. Choose from the range of large motifs on pages 96–122.

Medium-sized motifs These motifs can be effective when arranged in a pattern. Choose from the range of medium-sized motifs on pages 96–122.

Small motifs These small motifs are ideal for borders. Choose from the range of small motifs on pages 96–122.

Edging Select an edging from the Stitch Library, see pages 92–95. Choose from a wide range of cast-on borders and lace edgings. Follow the chart using the depth of the edging as a guide to the start point.

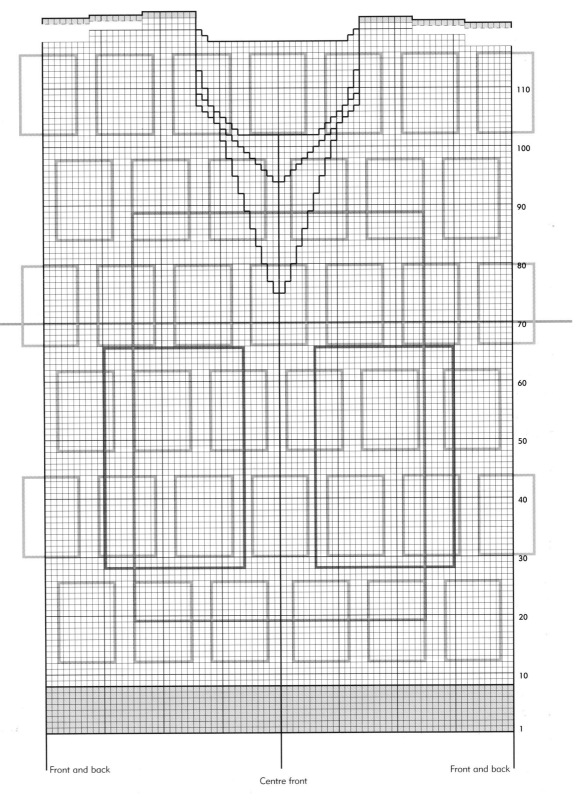

Front and back

Centre front

Front and back

CHART FOR CREWNECK AND V–NECK PULLOVER AND JACKET

Sleeves

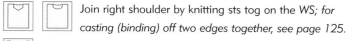

Cast on 42 sts using 3.25mm (US 3) needles. Work in moss st as given for back. *Alternatively work an edging of your choice, see pages 92–95.*

Change to 4mm (US 6) needles. Beg with a K row work in st st from chart. At the same time inc 1 st at each end of every 5th row to 64 sts rem. Work straight until sleeve measures 25cm (9¾in), ending with a WS row.

Cast off.

Finishing Pullover

Join right shoulder by knitting sts tog on the WS; *for casting (binding) off two edges together, see page 125.*

V NECKBAND

With RS facing and using 3.25mm (US 3) needles, pick up and K 30 sts down left side of front neck, 1 st at centre of V and mark this st, 30 sts up right side of front neck, 4 sts down right side of back neck, 24 sts from stitch holder at back of neck, 4 sts up left side of back neck. (93 sts.)

Work the neckband as follows or choose an alternative neckband or collar, see Style variations, pages 74–76.

Patt in moss st, work to within 2 sts of marked st, work 2 sts tog, K centre marked st, work next 2 sts tog, patt to end.

HOODED JACKET: *If you decide to add a hood to your garment, make sure that you buy an extra ball of yarn.*

Cont in rib as set, AT THE SAME TIME dec as set until band measures 3cm (1¼in).

Cast off loosely and evenly in patt.

Join left shoulder seam and neckband.

CREW NECKBAND

With RS facing pick up and K 20 sts down left side of front neck, 14 sts from stitch holder, 20 sts up right side of front neck, and 4 sts down right side of back neck, 24 sts from stitch holder, 4 sts up left side of back neck. (86 sts.)

Work the neckband as follows or choose an alternative neckband or collar, see Style Variations, pages 74–76.

Work in moss st for 3cm (1¼in), then cast off loosely and evenly in patt. Join left shoulder seam and neckband. *Alternatively work an edging of your choice; see pages 92–95.*

Finishing Jacket

Join both shoulders by knitting sts tog on the WS; *for casting (binding) off two edges together, see page 125.*

Finish the front bands or neckband as follows, or refer to Style variations, see pages 74–76, for an alternative neckband or collar.

V NECK FRONT BANDS

BUTTONHOLES: Make buttonholes on row 5. For a girl, on the right front band, patt 59 ▶ patt 2 sts tog, yo, patt 10 sts, rep from ▶ 3 more times, patt 2 sts tog, yo, patt 3. For a boy, on the left front band, patt 3 sts, ▶ yo, patt 2 sts tog, patt 10 sts, rep from ▶ 3 more times, yo, patt 2 sts tog, patt to end.

Right front band

With RS side facing, using 3.25mm (US 3) needles, beg at right front lower edge, pick up and K 56 sts up right front to beg of neck shaping, 40 sts up right side of neck, 4 sts down right side of back neck, 12 sts across to centre back of neck. (112 sts.)

For alternative fastenings and edgings, see Style variations, page 77.

Work in moss st for 8 rows. Cast off loosely and evenly in patt. *Alternatively work an edging of your choice, see pages 92–95.*

Left front band.

Work as given for Right front band, starting at Centre back neck.

For a contrast cast-off, see page 83.

CREW NECK FRONT BANDS

BUTTONHOLES: Make buttonholes on row 5. For a girl on the right front band and for a boy on the left front band. Patt 3 sts, ▶ yo, patt 2 sts tog, patt 12 sts, rep from ▶ 4 more times, yo, patt 2 sts tog, patt 3.

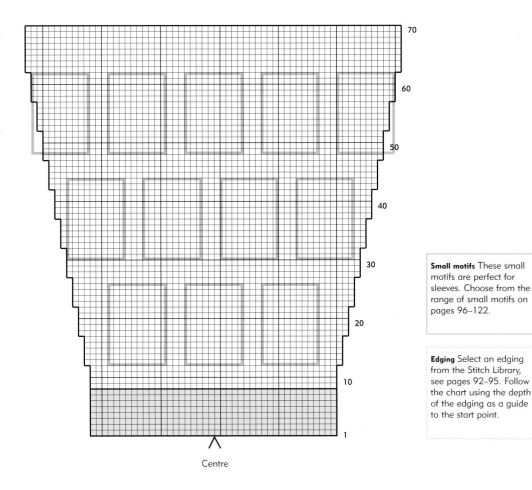

70

60

50

40

30

20

10

1

Centre

Small motifs These small motifs are perfect for sleeves. Choose from the range of small motifs on pages 96–122.

Edging Select an edging from the Stitch Library, see pages 92–95. Follow the chart using the depth of the edging as a guide to the start point.

CHART FOR SLEEVE FOR PULLOVER AND JACKET

Left front band

With RS facing and using 3.25mm (US 3) needles, pick up and K 78 sts along left front.

For alternative fastenings and edgings, see Style variations, page 77. Work in moss st for 8 rows. Cast off loosely and evenly in patt. *Alternatively work an edging of your choice, see pages 92–95.*

Right front band

Work as given for left front band.

For a contrast cast-off, see page 83.

Crew neckband

BUTTONHOLES: Depending on whether you are knitting for a boy or a girl, make a buttonhole on row 5 by either patt 2 sts, yo, patt 2 sts tog, patt to end, or patt to last 4 sts, patt 2 sts tog, yo, patt 2 sts. Beg at front edge of right front band and using 3.25mm (US 3) needles pick up and K 8 sts across band, 26 sts up right side of neck, 4 sts down right back neck, 24 sts across back of neck, 4 sts up left back neck 26 sts down left side of neck, 8 sts across left front band. (100 sts.) Work in moss st for 8 rows.

Cast off loosely and evenly in patt. *For a contrast cast-off, see page 83. Alternatively work an edging of your choice; see pages 92–95.*

Making Up

Press all pieces on WS with a warm iron over a damp cloth (or as instructions on yarn label), avoiding edging.

Join any alternative edging using a flat seam.

Using mattress stitch, sew in sleeves placing centre of cast off edge of sleeve to shoulder seam.

Join side and sleeve seams.

Press seams.

RIGHT: A classic look has been added to the V-neck jacket by working all the edgings in a K2, P2 rib with a stocking (stockinette) stitch roll *(see page 83)*. OPPOSITE: This crewneck pullover has a deep lacy edging *(see page 95)* added to the lower edge. A simple narrow picot edging *(see page 93)* has been added to the cuffs and neck.

CLASSIC GARMENT
5–6 YEARS

Chest 86cm (33¾in)

ACTUAL KNITTED MEASUREMENTS

Width at underarm	43cm (17in)
Length from shoulder	45cm (17¾in)
Length of sleeve	27cm (10½in)

YARNS

9 × 50g (1¾oz) balls of Rowan Handknit Cotton (photographed in light blue and deep pink); or an equivalent medium-weight cotton yarn. **Note:** *Extra yarn may be needed for style variations to the basic pattern, refer to pages 74–77 for additional yarn requirements.*

NEEDLES AND EXTRAS

1 pair 3.25mm (No.10/US 3) needles
1 pair 4mm (No.8/US 6) needles
Stitch holder
For V-neck jacket: 5 buttons
For crewneck jacket: 7 buttons

TENSION (GAUGE)

20 sts and 28 rows to 10cm (4in) measured over stocking (stockinette) stitch using 4mm (US 6) needles. If necessary, change needle size to obtain correct tension (gauge).

Back

Cast on 86 sts using 3.25mm (US 3) needles. *For a contrast cast-on, see page 83. Work the edging in moss (seed) stitch or see the Stitch library, pages 92–95, for an alternative edging.* Work in moss st as foll:

ROW 1: ▶ K1, P1, rep from ▶ to end.
ROW 2: ▶ P1, K1 rep from ▶ to end.
These 2 rows form moss st. Rep last 2 rows 3 times more
See Style variations, page 76, for Side vents.
Work the garment as follows, or see the Stitch library, pages 88–92, for an alternative stitch pattern.
Change to 4mm (US 6) needles. Beg with a K row work in st st from chart until work measures 45cm (17¾in), ending with a RS row. ▶
Shape shoulders
P77, wrap foll st, turn the work. *For short-row shaping see page 124.*
NEXT ROW: K21, turn, leaving rem sts on a holder.
NEXT ROW: P2tog, P10, wrap foll st. Turn the work.
NEXT ROW: K9, K2tog.
NEXT ROW: Work across all sts picking up loops of wrapped sts. Leave sts on a spare needle for shoulder seam.
With RS facing, return to rem 56 sts, slip centre 26 sts onto a stitch holder for back neck, rejoin yarn to rem 30 sts. K21, wrap foll st, turn the work. P19, P2tog.

5–6 YEARS

Chest 86cm (33¾in)

Back all pullovers and jackets

V-neck pullover

Crewneck pullover and jacket

V–neck pullover and jacket

Sleeve all pullovers and jackets

For information on:

Collars	pages 74–76
Fastenings	page 77
Hoods	pages 74–75
Panels	pages 76–77
Pockets	page 77
Side vents	page 76

NEXT ROW: K2tog, K9, wrap foll st, turn.

NEXT ROW: P10

Work across all sts picking up loops of wrapped sts.

Leave sts on a spare needle for shoulder seam.

Pullover Front

 V NECK

Work as given for back till work measures 24 rows less than the back, ending with a WS row.

Shape neck

Note: *Work the shorter V neckline on the chart for the pullover.*

Patt 43 sts, turn, leave rem sts on a holder.

Dec 1 st at neck edge on every row until 28 sts rem.

Work straight until work measures same as on back, ending with a RS row.

Shape shoulders

P19, wrap the next st, turn. *For short-row shaping see page 124.*

NEXT ROW: K19.

NEXT ROW: P10, wrap the next st, turn.

NEXT ROW: K10.

FOLL ROW: Work across all sts picking up loop of wrapped st.

Leave sts on a spare needle for shoulder seam.

Return to sts held on spare needle. Rejoin yarn and work 2nd side to match 1st side reversing all shaping.

CREW NECK

Work as given for back, until work measures 18 rows less than on back, ending with a WS row.

Shape neck

NEXT ROW: Patt 36 sts, leave rem sts on a spare needle, turn.

Dec 1 st at neck edge on every row until 28 sts rem. Work straight until work measures same as the back, ending with a RS row.

Shape shoulders

P19, wrap the next st, turn. *For short-row shaping see page 124.*

NEXT ROW: K19.

NEXT ROW: P10, wrap the next st, turn.

NEXT ROW: K10.

FOLL ROW: Work across all sts picking up loop of wrapped st.

Leave sts on a spare needle.

Return to sts held on a spare needle. Slip centre 14 sts onto a spare needle.

Rejoin yarn to rem 28 sts and work 2nd side to match 1st side reversing all shaping.

Jacket Left Front (V and crew neck)

 Cast on 43 sts using 3.25mm (US 3) needles. Work in moss st as given for back. *Alternatively work an edging of your choice, see pages 92–95. See Style variations, page 76, for Side vents.* Change to 4mm (US 6) needles. Beg with a K row work in st st from chart. Work until front measures 28cm (11in) ending with a RS row

V NECK

Shape front neck

Note: *Work the deeper V neckline on the chart for the jacket.*

NEXT ROW: Dec 1 st at beg of next row, work to end. Work 1 row.

Dec 1 st at neck edge on next and every foll 3rd row until 28 sts rem.

Work straight until work measures same as the back, ending with a RS row.

Shape shoulders

P19, wrap the next st, turn. *For short-row shaping see page 124.*

NEXT ROW: K19.

NEXT ROW: P10, wrap the next st, turn.

NEXT ROW: K10.

FOLL ROW: Work across all sts picking up loop of wrapped st.

Leave sts on a spare needle for shoulder seam.

CREW NECK

Work until front measures 16 rows less than on back, ending with a RS row.

Shape front neck

NEXT ROW: Cast off 7 sts, work to end

Dec 1 st at neck edge on every row until 28 sts rem.

Work straight until work measures same as back to shoulder, ending with a RS row.

Shape shoulders

P19, wrap the next st, turn. *For short-row shaping see page 124.*

NEXT ROW: K19.

NEXT ROW: P10, wrap the next st, turn.

NEXT ROW: K10.

FOLL ROW: Work across all sts picking up loop of wrapped st.

Leave sts on a spare needle for shoulder seam.

Jacket Right Front (V and crew neck)

 Work as given for left front, reversing all shaping.

Sleeves

Cast on 42 sts using 3.25mm (US 3) needles. Work in moss st as given for back. *Alternatively work an edging of your choice, see pages 92–95.*

Short-row shaping The orange highlighted row indicates the last row of short-row shaping, which is worked in order to hide the loop around the slipped stitch.

Collar Use a contrasting colour yarn to cast-off, see page 83, or consider one of the edgings on pages 92–95. Alternatively, select a different style of collar or neckband from the variations on pages 74–76.

Necklines The chart shows three neck lines, a crew-neck, a shallow V-neck and a deep V-neck. The deeper V-neck is ideal for jackets.

Position of buttons Mark the position of the buttons on the appropriate band. The first to come 1cm (½in) below the start of the neck shaping and the last to come 2 cm (¾in) from the cast on edge and the remainder to be spaced evenly between.

Yoke Consider introducing a change of colour or stitch detail at this point to create a yoke.

Buttons and bands Use a contrasting colour to cast off the bands to frame the front opening. Choose buttons that highlight the motifs used.

Central image If you are using a central motif, position it here. Choose from the range of large motifs on pages 96–122.

Medium-sized motifs These motifs can be effective when arranged in a pattern. Choose from the range of medium-sized motifs on pages 96–122.

Small motifs These small motifs are ideal for borders. Choose from the range of small motifs on pages 96–122.

Edging Select an edging from the Stitch Library, see pages 92–95. Choose from a wide range of cast-on borders and lace edgings. Follow the chart using the depth of the edging as a guide to the start point.

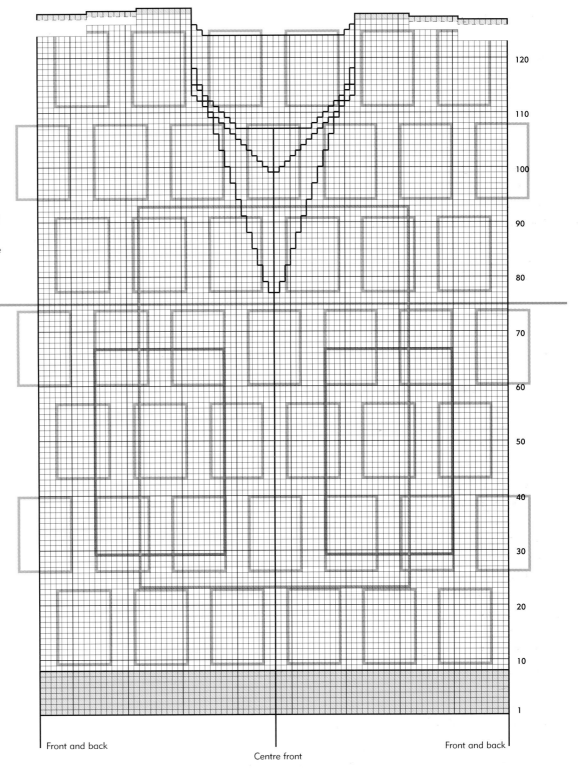

Front and back

Centre front

Front and back

CHART FOR CREWNECK AND V–NECK PULLOVER AND JACKET

Change to 4mm (US 6) needles. Beg with a K row work in st st from chart. At the same time inc 1 st at each end of every 5th row until 68 sts rem. Work straight until sleeve measures 27cm (10½in), ending with a WS row.
Cast off.

Finishing Pullover

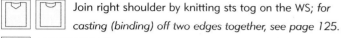 Join right shoulder by knitting sts tog on the WS; *for casting (binding) off two edges together, see page 125.*

V NECKBAND

With RS facing and using 3.25mm (US 3) needles, pick up and K 30 sts down left side of front neck, 1 st at centre of V and mark this st, 30 sts up right side of front neck, 4 sts down right side of back neck, 26 sts from stitch holder, and 4 sts up left side of back neck. (95 sts.)
Work the neckband as follows or choose an alternative neckband or collar, see Style variations, pages 74–76.
Patt in moss st, work to within 2 sts of marked st, work 2 sts tog, K centre marked st, work next 2 sts tog, patt to end.
Cont in rib as set, AT THE SAME TIME dec as set until band measures 3cm (1¼in).

MIXING PATTERNS: *If you want to mix a lace edging with a patterned cast-off detail then make sure that they suit each other.*

Cast off loosely and evenly in patt.
Join left shoulder seam and neckband.

CREW NECKBAND

With RS facing pick up and K 23 sts down left side of front neck, 14 sts from stitch holder, 23 sts up left side of front neck, 4 sts down left side of back neck, 26 sts from stitch holder, and 4 sts up right side of back neck. (94 sts.)
Work the neckband as follows or choose an alternative neckband or collar, see Style variations, pages 74–76.
Work in moss st for 3cm (1¼in), then cast off loosely and evenly in patt. Join left shoulder seam and neckband. *Alternatively work an edging of your choice; see pages 92–95.*

Finishing Jacket

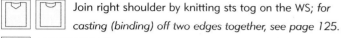 Join both shoulders by knitting sts tog on the WS; *for casting (binding) off two edges together, see page 125.*
Finish the front bands or neckband as follows, or refer to Style variations, see pages 74–76, for an alternative neckband or collar.

V NECK FRONT BANDS

BUTTONHOLES: Make buttonholes on row 5. For a girl, on the right front band, patt 64 ▶ patt 2 sts tog, yo, patt 10 sts, rep from ▶ 3 more times, patt 2 sts tog, yo, patt 3. For a boy, on the left front band, patt 3 sts, ▶ yo, patt 2 sts tog, patt 10 sts, rep from ▶ 3 more times, yo, patt 2 sts tog, patt to end.

Right front band

With RS side facing, using 3.25mm (US 3) needles, beg at right front lower edge, pick up and K 57 sts up right front to beg of neck shaping, 43 sts up right side of neck, 4 sts down right side of back neck, 13 sts across to centre back of neck. (117 sts.)
For alternative fastenings and edgings, see Style variations, page 77.
Work in moss st for 8 rows. Cast off loosely and evenly in patt.
Alternatively work an edging of your choice, see pages 92–95.

Left front band

Work as given for Right front band, starting at Centre back neck.
For a contrast cast-off, see page 83.

CREW NECK FRONT BANDS

BUTTONHOLES: Make buttonholes on row 5. For a girl on the right front band and for a boy on the left front band. Patt 3 sts, ▶ yo, patt 2 sts tog, patt 12 sts, rep from ▶ 4 more times, yo, patt 2 sts tog, patt 3.

Left front band

With RS facing and using 3.25mm (US 3) needles, pick up and K 78 sts along left front.
For alternative fastenings and edgings, see Style variations, page 77.

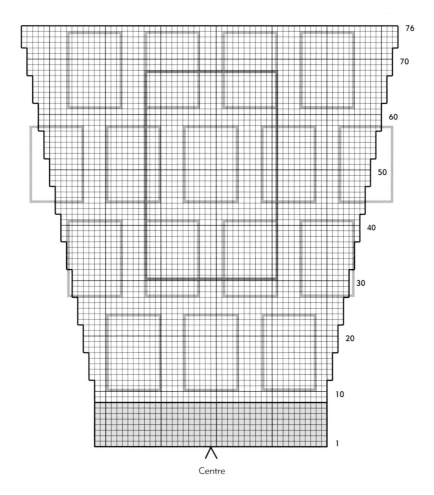

76
70
60
50
40
30
20
10
1

↑
Centre

**CHART FOR SLEEVE FOR
PULLOVER AND JACKET**

Medium-sized motifs Choose from the range of medium-sized motifs on pages 96–122.

Small motifs These small motifs are perfect for sleeves. Choose from the range of small motifs on pages 96–122.

Edging Select an edging from the Stitch Library, see pages 92–95. Follow the chart using the depth of the edging as a guide to the start point.

Work in moss st for 8 rows. Cast off loosely and evenly in patt.
Alternatively work an edging of your choice, see pages 92–95.
Right front band
Work as given for left front band.
For a contrast cast-off, see page 83.
Crew neckband
BUTTONHOLES: Depending on whether you are knitting for a boy or a girl, make a buttonhole on row 5 by either patt 2 sts, yo, patt 2 sts tog, patt to end, or patt to last 4 sts, patt 2 sts tog, yo, patt 2 sts.
Beg at front edge of right front band and using 3.25mm (US 3) needles pick up and K 8 sts across band, 29 sts up right side of neck, 4 sts down right back neck, 26 sts across back of neck, 4 sts up left back neck, 29 sts down left side of neck, and 8 sts across left front band. (108 sts.)

Work in moss st for 8 rows.
Cast off loosely and evenly in patt. *For a contrast cast-off, see page 83.*
Alternatively work an edging of your choice; see pages 92–95.

Making up

Press all pieces on WS with a warm iron over a damp cloth (or as instructions on yarn label), avoiding edging.
Join any alternative edging using a flat seam.
Using mattress stitch, sew in sleeves placing centre of cast off edge of sleeve to shoulder seam.
Join side and sleeve seams.
Press seams.

RIGHT: A V-neck jacket, knitted in pale yellow. Moss (seed) stitch lapels *(see page 76)* have been added to the front neck shaping. OPPOSITE: This crewneck pullover, knitted in mid green, has been given a smart look by adding a high neckline with a zip fastener *(see page 74)* and a pocket on the left sleeve *(see page 77)*. All edging has been worked in K2, P2 rib with a stocking (stockinette) stitch roll *(see page 77)*.

CLASSIC GARMENT
7–8 YEARS

Chest 90cm (35½in)

ACTUAL KNITTED MEASUREMENTS

Width at underarm	45cm (17¾in)
Length from shoulder	48cm (19in)
Length of sleeve	32cm (12½in)

YARNS

10 × 50g (1¾oz) balls of Rowan Handknit Cotton (photographed in mid green and pale yellow); or an equivalent medium-weight cotton yarn. **Note:** *Extra yarn may be needed for style variations to the basic pattern, refer to pages 74–77 for additional yarn requirements.*

NEEDLES AND EXTRAS

1 pair 3.25mm (No.10/US 3) needles
1 pair 4mm (No.8/US 6) needles
Stitch holder
For V-neck jacket: 5 buttons
For crewneck jacket: 7 buttons

TENSION (GAUGE)

20 sts and 28 rows to 10cm (4in) measured over stocking (stockinette) stitch using 4mm (US 6) needles. If necessary, change needle size to obtain correct tension (gauge).

Back

Cast on 90sts using 3.25mm (US 3) needles. *For a contrast cast-on, see page 83. Work the edging in moss (seed) stitch or see the Stitch library, pages 92–95, for an alternative edging.* Work in moss st as foll:

ROW 1: ▶ K1, P1, rep from ▶ to end.
ROW 2: ▶ P1, K1, rep from ▶ to end.
These 2 rows form moss st. Rep last 2 rows 2 times more.
See Style variations, page 76, for Side vents.
Work the garment as follows, or see the Stitch library, pages 88–92, for an alternative stitch pattern.
Change to 4mm (US 6) needles. Beg with a K row work in st st from chart until work measures 29.5cm (11½in), ending with a WS row. ▶
Shape armhole
Cast off 4 sts at beg of next 2 rows.
Dec 1 st at each end of next 6 rows (70 sts). ▶▶
Work straight until armhole measures 18.5cm (7¼in) ending with a RS row.
Shape shoulders
P60, wrap foll st, turn the work. *For short-row shaping see page 124.*
NEXT ROW: K11, turn, leaving rem sts on a holder.
NEXT ROW: P2tog, work across all sts picking up loops of wrapped sts.
Leave sts on a spare needle for shoulder seam. With RS facing, return to rem 49 sts, slip centre 28 sts onto a stitch holder for back neck,

**Back all pullovers
and jackets**

V-neck pullover

**Crewneck pullover
and jacket**

**V–neck pullover
and jacket**

**Sleeve all pullovers
and jackets**

For information on:

Collars	pages 74–76
Fastenings	page 77
Hoods	pages 74–75
Panels	pages 76–77
Pockets	page 77
Side vents	page 76

rejoin yarn to rem 21 sts. K11, wrap foll st, turn the work, P9, P2tog, work across all sts picking up loop of wrapped st. Leave sts on a spare needle for shoulder seam.

Pullover Front

 V NECK

Work as given for back to ▶▶.

Work straight until front measures 30 rows less than back, ending with a WS row.

Shape neck

Note: Work the shorter V neckline on the chart for the pullover.

Patt 35 sts, turn, leave rem sts on a holder.

Dec 1 st at neck edge on next and every foll 3rd row until 19 sts rem.

Cont straight until work measures the same as the back, ending with a RS row

Shape shoulders

P9, wrap the next st, turn. *For short-row shaping see page 124.*

NEXT ROW: K9.

FOLL ROW: Work across all sts picking up loop of wrapped st.

Leave sts on a spare needle for shoulder seam.

Return to rem 35 sts held on spare needle. Rejoin yarn and work to match first side, reversing all shaping.

Leave sts on a spare needle for shoulder seam.

 CREW NECK

Work as given for back to ▶▶.

Work straight until armhole measures 20 rows less than on back, ending with a WS row.

Shape neck

NEXT ROW: Patt 28 sts, leave rem sts on a spare needle, turn.

Dec 1 st at neck edge on every row until 19 sts rem. Work straight until armhole measures same as the back, ending with a RS row.

Shape shoulders

P9, wrap the next st, turn. *For short-row shaping see page 124.*

NEXT ROW: K9.

FOLL ROW: Work across all sts picking up loop of wrapped st.

Leave rem 19 sts on a spare needle for shoulder seam.

With RS facing, return to rem sts held on a spare needle; slip centre 14 sts onto a stitch holder for front neck. Rejoin yarn and work second side to match first side reversing shaping.

Jacket Left Front (V and crew neck)

 Cast on 45 sts using 3.25mm (US 3) needles. Work in moss st as given for back. *Alternatively work an edging*

of your choice, see pages 92–95.

See Style variations, page 76, for Side vents.

Change to 4mm (US 6) needles. Beg with a K row work in st st from chart until work measures 29.5cm (11½in) ending with a WS row.

 V NECK

Shape armholes and front neck

Note: Work the deeper V neckline on the chart for the jacket.

NEXT ROW: Cast off 4 sts, work to last 2 sts, K2tog.

NEXT ROW: Work across sts.

NEXT ROW: Dec 1 st at each end of next row.

Cont to dec 1 st at neck edge on every foll 3rd row and AT THE SAME TIME, dec 1 st at the armhole edge on the next 5 rows. (32 sts.) Cont dec neck edge until 19 sts rem. Work straight until armhole measures same as on back.

Shape shoulders

P9, wrap the next st, turn. *For short-row shaping see page 124.*

NEXT ROW: K9.

FOLL ROW: Work across all sts picking up loop of wrapped st.

Leave rem 19 sts on a spare needle for shoulder seam.

CREW NECK

Shape armholes and front neck

NEXT ROW: Cast off 4 sts at beg of next row.

NEXT ROW: Dec 1 st at armhole edge on next 6 rows.

Work straight until armhole measures 21 rows less than on back, ending with a RS row.

Cast off 7 sts at beg of next row, work to end.

Dec 1 st at neck edge on every row until 19 sts rem.

Work straight until armhole measures same as on back to shoulder.

Shape shoulders

P9, wrap the next st, turn. *For short-row shaping see page 124.*

NEXT ROW: K9.

FOLL ROW: Work across all sts picking up loop of wrapped st.

Hold sts on a spare needle for shoulder seam.

Jacket Right Front (V and crew neck)

Work as given for left front, reversing all shaping.

Sleeves

Cast on 42 sts using 3.25mm (US 3) needles. Work in moss st as given for back. *Alternatively work an edging of your choice, see pages 92–95.*

Change to 4mm (US 6) needles. Beg with a K row work in st st from

Short-row shaping The orange highlighted row indicates the last row of short-row shaping, which is worked in order to hide the loop around the slipped stitch.

Collar Use a contrasting colour yarn to cast-off, see page 83, or consider one of the edgings on pages 92–95. Alternatively, select a different style of collar or neckband from the variations on pages 74–76.

Necklines The chart shows three neck lines, a crew-neck, a shallow V-neck and a deep V-neck. The deeper V-neck is ideal for jackets.

Position of buttons Mark the position of the buttons on the appropriate band. The first to come 1cm (½in) below the start of the neck shaping and the last to come 2 cm (¾in) from the cast on edge and the remainder to be spaced evenly between.

Yoke Consider introducing a change of colour or stitch detail at this point to create a yoke.

Buttons and bands Use a contrasting colour to cast off the bands to frame the front opening.

Central image If you are using a central motif, position it here. Choose from the range of large motifs on pages 96–122.

Medium-sized motifs These motifs can be effective when arranged in a pattern. Choose from the range of medium-sized motifs on pages 96–122.

Small motifs These small motifs are ideal for borders. Choose from the range of small motifs on pages 96–122.

Edging Select an edging from the Stitch Library, see pages 92–95. Choose from a wide range of cast-on borders and lace edgings. Follow the chart using the depth of the edging as a guide to the start point.

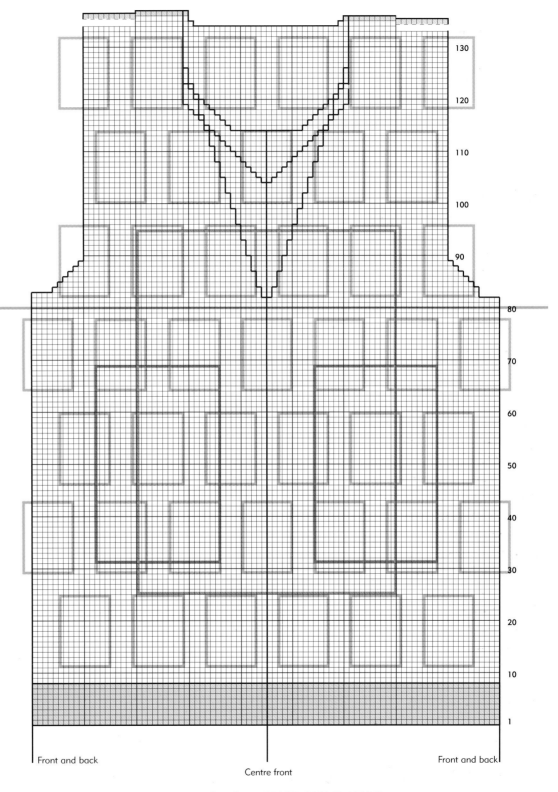

Front and back

Centre front

Front and back

**CHART FOR CREWNECK AND V–NECK
PULLOVER AND JACKET**

chart. At the same time inc 1 st at each end of every 5th row to 74 sts . Work straight until sleeve measures 32cm (12½in), ending with a WS row.

Shape sleeve head (cap)

Cast off 4 sts at the beg of next 2 rows (66 sts). Dec 1 st at each end of next 6 rows (54 sts). Cast off.

Finishing Pullover

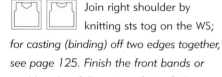 Join right shoulder by knitting sts tog on the WS; *for casting (binding) off two edges together, see page 125. Finish the front bands or neckband as follows, or refer to Style variations, see pages 74–76, for an alternative neckband or collar.*

V NECKBAND

With RS facing and using 3.25mm (US 3) needles, pick up and K 35 sts down left side of front neck, 1 st at centre of V and mark this st, 35 sts up right side of front neck, 6 sts down right side of back neck, 28 sts from stitch holder and 6 sts up left side of back neck. (111 sts.)

Work the neckband as follows or choose an alternative neckband or collar, see Style variations, pages 74–76.

Patt in K1, P1 rib, work to within 2 sts of marked st, work 2 sts tog, K centre marked st, work next 2 sts tog, patt to end.

Cont in rib and dec as set for 8 rows.

Cast off loosely and evenly in rib. Join left shoulder seam and neckband.

CREW NECKBAND

With RS facing pick up and K 26 sts down left side of front neck, 14 sts from stitch holder, 26 sts up left side of front neck, 6 sts down right side of back neck, 28 sts from stitch holder and 6 sts up left side of back neck. (106 sts.)

Work the neckband as follows or choose an alternative neckband or collar, see Style variations, pages 74–76.

Work in moss st for 8 rows.

Cast off loosely and evenly in patt. Join left shoulder seam and neckband. *Alternatively work an edging of your choice; see pages 92–95.*

Finishing Jacket

Join both shoulders by knitting sts tog on the WS; *for casting (binding) off two edges together, see page 125.*

COMFORTABLE DESIGN: If you like the style of a high neckband but your child finds it too constricting to wear, choose a high neckband with a zip fastening for a more comfortable alternative.

V NECK FRONT BANDS

BUTTONHOLES: Make buttonholes on row 5. For a girl, on the right front band, patt 74 ▶ patt 2 sts tog, yo, patt 11 sts, rep from ▶ 3 more times, patt 2 sts tog, yo, patt 3. For a boy, on the left front band, patt 3 sts, ▶ yo, patt 2 sts tog, patt 11 sts, rep from ▶ 3 more times, yo, patt 2 sts tog, patt to end.

Right front band

With RS side facing, using 3.25mm (US 3) needles, beg at right front lower edge, pick up and K 60 sts up right front to beg of neck shaping, 51 sts up right side of neck, 6 sts down right side of back neck, 14 sts across to centre back of neck. (131 sts.)

For alternative fastenings and edgings, see Style variations, page 77. Work in moss st for 8 rows. Cast off loosely and evenly in patt. Alternatively work an edging of your choice, see pages 92–95.

Left front band

Work as given for Right front band, starting at Centre back neck.

For a contrast cast-off, see page 83.

CREW NECK FRONT BANDS

BUTTONHOLES: Make buttonholes on row 5. For a girl on the right front band and for a boy on the left front band. Patt 3 sts, ▶ yo, patt 2 sts tog, patt 13 sts, rep from ▶ 4 more times, yo, patt 2 sts tog, patt 3.

Left front band

With RS facing and using 3.25mm (US 3) needles, pick up and K 83 sts along left front.

For alternative fastenings and edgings, see Style variations, page 77. Work in moss st for 8 rows. Cast off loosely and evenly in patt. *Alternatively work an edging of your choice, see pages 92–95.*

Right front band

Work as given for left front band.

For a contrast cast-off, see page 83.

Crew neckband

BUTTONHOLES: Depending on whether you are knitting for a boy or a

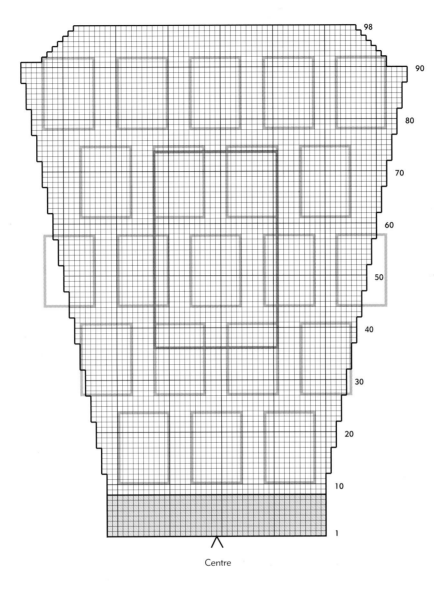

98
90
80
70
60
50
40
30
20
10
1

Centre

**CHART FOR SLEEVE FOR
PULLOVER AND JACKET**

Medium-sized motifs Choose from the range of medium-sized motifs on pages 96–122.

Small motifs These small motifs are perfect for sleeves. Choose from the range of small motifs on pages 96–122.

Edging Select an edging from the Stitch Library, see pages 92–95. Follow the chart using the depth of the edging as a guide to the start point.

girl, make a buttonhole on row 5 by either patt 2 sts, yo, patt 2 sts tog, patt to end, or patt to last 4 sts, patt 2 sts tog, yo, patt 2 sts. Beg at front edge of right front band and using 3.25mm (US 3) needles pick up and K 8 sts across band, 33 sts up right side of neck, 6 sts down right back neck, 28 sts across back of neck, 4 sts up left back neck 33 sts down left side of neck, 6 sts across left front band. (122 sts.)

Work in moss st for 8 rows.

Cast off loosely and evenly in patt. *For a contrast cast-off, see page 83. Alternatively work an edging of your choice; see pages 92–95.*

Making Up

Press all pieces on WS with a warm iron over a damp cloth (or as instructions on yarn label), avoiding edging.

Join any alternative edging using a flat seam.

Using mattress stitch, sew in sleeves by joining cast-off sts at the beg of the armhole shaping to cast-off sts at start of sleeve-head shaping. Sew sleeve-head into armhole, easing in shaping.

Join side and sleeve seams.

Press seams.

RIGHT: As simple as you can get, this V-neck pullover has stocking (stockinette) stitch edgings *(see page 74)* on neck shaping, lower edges and sleeves. OPPOSITE: This crewneck jacket has a reverse stocking (stockinette) stitch yoke and small pocket flaps *(see page 77)*. The cuffs have been folded in half and secured with a button *(see page 77)*.

CLASSIC GARMENT
9–10 YEARS
Chest 96cm (37¾in)

ACTUAL KNITTED MEASUREMENTS

Width at underarm	48cm (19in)
Length from shoulder	52cm (20½in)
Length of sleeve	34cm (13½in)

YARNS

11 × 50g (1¾oz) balls of Rowan Handknit Cotton (photographed in navy blue and pale grey); or an equivalent medium-weight cotton yarn. **Note:** *Extra yarn may be needed for style variations to the basic pattern, refer to pages 74–77 for additional yarn requirements.*

NEEDLES AND EXTRAS

1 pair 3.25mm (No.10/US 3) needles
1 pair 4mm (No.8/US 6) needles
Stitch holder
For V-neck jacket: 5 buttons
For crewneck jacket: 7 buttons

TENSION (GAUGE)

20 sts and 28 rows to 10cm (4in) measured over stocking (stockinette) stitch using 4mm (US 6) needles. If necessary, change needle size to obtain correct tension (gauge).

Back

Cast on 96 sts using 3.25mm (US 3) needles. *For a contrast cast-on, see page 83. Work the edging in moss (seed) stitch or see the Stitch library, pages 92–95, for an alternative edging.* Work in moss st as foll:

ROW 1: ▶ K1, P1, rep from ▶ to end.
ROW 2: ▶ P1, K1, rep from ▶ to end.
These 2 rows form moss st. Rep last 2 rows 3 times more
See Style variations, page 76, for Side vents.
Work the garment as follows, or see the Stitch library, pages 88–92, for an alternative stitch pattern.
Change to 4mm (US 6) needles. Beg with a K row work in st st from chart until work measures 52cm (20½in), ending with a RS row. ▶

Shape shoulders

P86, wrap foll st, turn the work. *For short-row shaping see page 124.*
NEXT ROW: K24, turn, leaving rem sts on a holder.
NEXT ROW: P2tog, P12, wrap foll st, turn the work.
NEXT ROW: K10, K2tog, turn.
NEXT ROW: Work across all sts picking up loops of wrapped sts.
Leave sts on a spare needle for shoulder seam.
With RS facing, return to rem 62 sts, slip centre 28 sts onto a stitch holder for back neck, rejoin yarn to rem 34 sts.
K24, wrap foll st, turn the work.

CLASSIC GARMENT
9–10 YEARS

Chest 96cm (37¾in)

**Back all pullovers
and jackets**

V-neck pullover

**Crewneck pullover
and jacket**

**V–neck pullover
and jacket**

**Sleeve all pullovers
and jackets**

For information on:

Collars	pages 74–76
Fastenings	page 77
Hoods	pages 74–75

NEXT ROW: P22, P2tog.

NEXT ROW: K2tog, K11, wrap foll st, turn.

NEXT ROW: P12.

NEXT ROW: Work across all sts picking up loops of wrapped sts.

Leave sts on a spare needle for shoulder seam.

Pullover Front

 V NECK

Work as given for back till work measures 28 rows less than the back, ending with a WS row.

Shape neck

Note: *Work the shorter V neckline on the chart for the pullover.*

Patt 48 sts, turn, leave rem sts on a holder.

Dec 1 st at neck edge on every row until 32 sts rem.

Work straight until work measures same as on back, ending with a RS row.

Shape shoulders

P22, wrap the next st, turn. *For short-row shaping see page 124.*

NEXT ROW: K22.

NEXT ROW: P12, wrap the next st, turn.

NEXT ROW: K12.

FOLL ROW: Work across all sts picking up loop of wrapped st.

Leave sts on a spare needle for shoulder seam.

Return to sts held on spare needle. Rejoin yarn and work 2nd side to match 1st side reversing all shaping.

 CREW NECK

Work as given for back, until work measures 20 rows less than on back, ending with a WS row.

Shape neck

NEXT ROW: Patt 41 sts, leave rem sts on a spare needle, turn.

Dec 1 st at neck edge on every row until 32 sts rem. Work straight until work measures same as the back, ending with a RS row.

Shape shoulders

P22, wrap the next st, turn. *For short-row shaping see page 124.*

NEXT ROW: K22.

NEXT ROW: P12, wrap the next st, turn.

NEXT ROW: K12.

FOLL ROW: Work across all sts picking up loop of wrapped st.

Leave sts on a spare needle.

Return to sts held on a spare needle. Slip centre 14 sts onto a spare needle.

Rejoin yarn to rem 41 sts and work 2nd side to match 1st side reversing all shaping.

SIMPLE STYLE: *Stocking (stockinette) stitch edgings give a very modern casual look to an easy-to-wear sweater.*

Jacket Left Front (V and crew neck)

 Cast on 48 sts using 3.25mm (US 3) needles. Work in moss st as given for back. *Alternatively work an edging of your choice, see pages 92–95.*

See Style variations, page 76, for Side vents.

Change to 4mm (US 6) needles. Beg with a K row work in st st from chart.

V NECK

Work until measures 31cm (12¾in) ending with a RS row.

Shape front neck

Note: *Work the deeper V neckline on the chart for the jacket.*

NEXT ROW: Dec 1 st at beg of next row, work to end. Work 1 row

Dec 1 st at neck edge on next and every foll 3rd row until 32 sts rem.

Work straight until work measures same as the back, ending with a RS row.

Shape shoulders

P22, wrap the next st, turn. *For short-row shaping see page 124.*

NEXT ROW: K22.

NEXT ROW: P12, wrap the next st, turn.

NEXT ROW: K12.

FOLL ROW: Work across all sts picking up loop of wrapped st.

Leave sts on a spare needle for shoulder seam.

CREW NECK

Work until front measures 21 rows less than on back, ending with a RS row.

Short-row shaping The orange highlighted row indicates the last row of short-row shaping, which is worked in order to hide the loop around the slipped stitch.

Collar Use a contrasting colour yarn to cast-off, see page 83, or consider one of the edgings on pages 92–95. Alternatively, select a different style of collar or neckband from the variations on pages 74–76.

Necklines The chart shows three neck lines, a crew-neck, a shallow V-neck and a deep V-neck. The deeper V-neck is ideal for jackets.

Position of buttons Mark the position of the buttons on the appropriate band. The first to come 1cm (½in) below the start of the neck shaping and the last to come 2 cm (¾in) from the cast on edge and the remainder to be spaced evenly between.

Yoke Consider introducing a change of colour or stitch detail at this point to create a yoke.

Buttons and bands Use a contrasting colour to cast off the bands to frame the front opening.

Central image If you are using a central motif, position it here. Choose from the range of large motifs on pages 96–122.

Medium-sized motifs These motifs can be effective when arranged in a pattern. Choose from the range of medium-sized motifs on pages 96–122.

Small motifs These small motifs are ideal for borders. Choose from the range of small motifs on pages 96–122.

Edging Select an edging from the Stitch Library, see pages 92–95. Choose from a wide range of cast-on borders and lace edgings. Follow the chart using the depth of the edging as a guide to the start point.

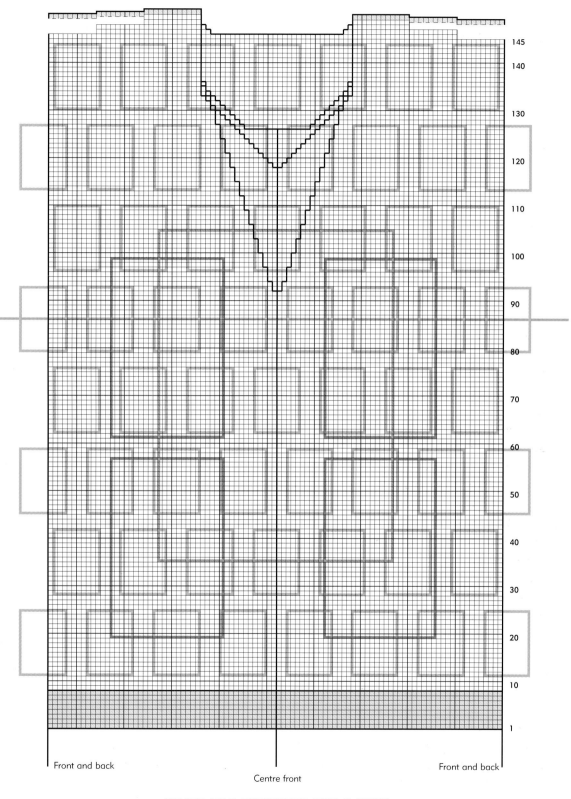

Front and back

Centre front

Front and back

CHART FOR CREWNECK AND V–NECK PULLOVER AND JACKET

Shape front neck

NEXT ROW: Cast off 7 sts, work to end

Dec 1 st at neck edge on every row until 32 sts.

Work straight until work measures same as back to shoulder, ending with a RS row.

Shape shoulders

P22, wrap the next st, turn. *For short-row shaping see page 124.*

NEXT ROW: K22.

NEXT ROW: P12, wrap the next st, turn.

NEXT ROW: K12.

FOLL ROW: Work across all sts picking up loop of wrapped st.

Leave sts on a spare needle for shoulder seam.

Jacket Right Front (V and crew neck)

  Work as given for left front, reversing all shaping.

Sleeves

 Cast on 46 sts using 3.25mm (US 3) needles. Work in moss st as given for back. *Alternatively work an edging of your choice, see pages 92–95.*

Change to 4mm (US 6) needles. Beg with a K row work in st st from chart. At the same time inc 1 st at each end of every 5th row to 80 sts. Work straight until sleeve measures 34cm (13½in), ending with a WS row.

Cast off.

Finishing Pullover

  Join right shoulder by knitting sts tog on the WS; *for casting (binding) off two edges together, see page 125.*

V NECKBAND

With RS facing and using 3.25mm (US 3) needles, pick up and K 37 sts down left side of front neck, 1 st at centre of V and mark this st, 37 sts up right side of front neck, 5 sts down right side of back neck, 28 sts from stitch holder, 5 sts up left side of back neck. (113 sts.)

Work the neckband as follows or choose an alternative neckband or collar, see Style variations, pages 74–76.

Patt in moss st, work to within 2 sts of marked st, work 2 sts tog, K centre marked st, work next 2 sts tog, patt to end.

Cont in rib as set, AT THE SAME TIME dec as set until 8 rows have been worked.

Cast off loosely and evenly in patt.

Join left shoulder seam and neckband.

CREW NECKBAND

With RS facing pick up and K 25 sts down left side of front neck, 14 sts from stitch holder, 25 sts up left side of front neck, and 5 sts down left side of back neck, 28 sts from stitch holder, 5 sts up right side of back neck. (102 sts.)

Work the neckband as follows or choose an alternative neckband or collar, see Style variations, pages 74–76.

Work in moss st for 8 rows. Cast off loosely and evenly in patt. Join left shoulder seam and neckband.

Alternatively work an edging of your choice; see pages 92–95.

Finishing Jacket

Join both shoulders by knitting sts tog on the WS; *for casting (binding) off two edges together, see page 125.*

Finish the front bands or neckband as follows, or refer to Style variations, see pages 74–76, for an alternative neckband or collar.

V NECK FRONT BANDS

BUTTONHOLES: Make buttonholes on row 5. For a girl, on the right front band, patt 75 ▶ patt 2 sts tog, yo, patt 13 sts, rep from ▶ 3 more times, patt 2 sts tog, yo, patt 3. For a boy, on the left front band, patt 3 sts, ▶ yo, patt 2 sts tog, patt 13 sts, rep from ▶ 3 more times, yo, patt 2 sts tog, patt to end.

Right front band

With RS side facing, using 3.25mm (US 3) needles, beg at right front lower edge, pick up and K 68 sts up right front to beg of neck shaping, 53 sts up right side of neck, 5 sts down right side of back neck, 14 sts across to centre back of neck. (140 sts.)

For alternative fastenings and edgings, see Style variations, page 77.

Work in moss st for 8 rows. Cast off loosely and evenly in patt.

Alternatively work an edging of your choice, see pages 92–95.

Left front band.

Work as given for Right front band, starting at Centre back neck.

For a contrast cast-off, see page 83.

CREW NECK FRONT BANDS

BUTTONHOLES: Make buttonholes on row 5. For a girl on the right front band and for a boy on the left front band. Patt 3 sts, ▶ yo, patt 2 sts tog, patt 15 sts, rep from ▶ 4 more times, yo, patt 2 sts tog, patt 3.

Left front band

With RS facing and using 3.25mm (US 3) needles, pick up and K 93 sts along left front.

For alternative fastenings and edgings, see Style variations, page 77.

Work in moss st for 8 rows. Cast off loosely and evenly in patt.

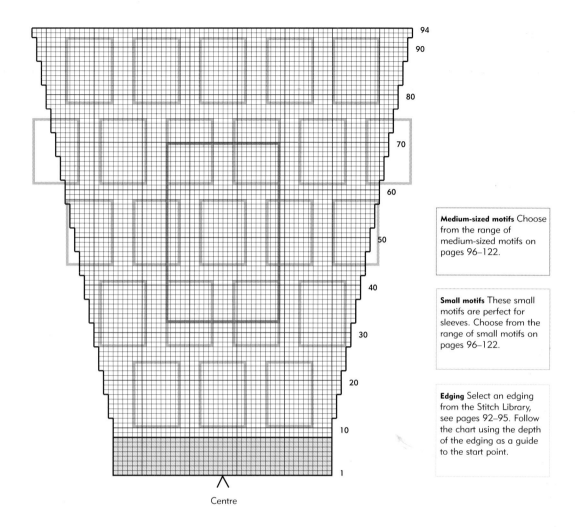

94
90
80
70
60
50
40
30
20
10
1

Centre

Medium-sized motifs Choose from the range of medium-sized motifs on pages 96–122.

Small motifs These small motifs are perfect for sleeves. Choose from the range of small motifs on pages 96–122.

Edging Select an edging from the Stitch Library, see pages 92–95. Follow the chart using the depth of the edging as a guide to the start point.

CHART FOR SLEEVE FOR PULLOVER AND JACKET

Alternatively work an edging of your choice, see pages 92–95.

Right front band

Work as given for left front band.

For a contrast cast-off, see page 83.

Crew neckband

BUTTONHOLES: Depending on whether you are knitting for a boy or a girl, make a buttonhole on row 5 by either patt 2 sts, yo, patt 2 sts tog, patt to end, or patt to last 4 sts, patt 2 sts tog, yo, patt 2 sts.
Beg at front edge of right front band and using 3.25mm (US 3) needles pick up and K 8 sts across band, 31 sts up right side of neck, 5 sts down right back neck, 28 sts across back of neck, 5 sts up left back neck 31 sts down left side of neck, and 8 sts across left front band. (116 sts.)

Work in moss st for 8 rows.

Cast off loosely and evenly in patt. *For a contrast cast-off, see page 83. Alternatively work an edging of your choice; see pages 92–95.*

Making Up

Press all pieces on WS with a warm iron over a damp cloth (or as instructions on yarn label), avoiding edging.
Join any alternative edging using a flat seam.
Using mattress stitch, sew in sleeves placing centre of cast off edge of sleeve to shoulder seam.
Join side and sleeve seams.
Press seams.

RIGHT: Knit this hat with or without a tassel or you can add a pompon to turn the hat into a christmas gift. The depth of the brim can be made shallower if no motifs are to be worked.

CLASSIC GARMENT
HAT
WITH BRIM

To fit 2–3 (4–6, 7–10) years

TO FIT
Ages   2–3 (4–6:7–10) years

YARN
2(3:3) × 50g (1¾oz) balls of Rowan Handknit Cotton (photographed in deep orange); or an equivalent medium weight cotton yarn

NEEDLES AND EXTRAS
1 pair 3.25mm (No10/US 3) needles
1 pair 4mm (No 8/US 6) needles.

TENSION (GAUGE)
20 sts and 28 rows to 10cm (4in) measured over stocking (stockinette) stitch using 4mm (US 6) needles. If necessary, change needles size to obtain correct tension (gauge).

Hat

Cast on 72(86:100) sts using 3.25mm (US 3) needles. Work in moss st for 3(5:7) rows.
Change to 4mm (US 6) needles. Beg with a K row work 18 rows in st st.
Work a further 3(5:7) rows in moss st.
Beg with a K row work in st st for 24(28:32) rows.
SHAPE CROWN:
K4(6:8), ▶ K2tog, K2tog tbl, K8(10:12), rep from ▶ to last 8(10:12) sts, K2tog, K2tog tbl, K4(6:8). [60(74:88) sts.]
NEXT ROW: Purl.
NEXT ROW: Knit.
NEXT ROW: Purl.
FOLL ROW: K3(5:7), ▶ K2tog, K2tog tbl, K6(8:10), rep from ▶ to last 7(9:11) sts, K2tog, K2tog tbl, K3(5:7).
Cont to dec as set on every 4th row until 12(14:16) sts rem. Slip yarn back through rem sts and fasten off.

Making Up

Join hat seam and fold the brim back at point of moss st border and reverse seam. Make tassel for top of hat and sew into place at centre of crown.

Front and back

To fit 2–3 (4–6, 7–10) years

Edging Select an edging from the Stitch Library, see pages 92–95. Follow the chart using the depth of the edging as a guide to the start point.

Small motifs These small motifs are perfect for brim. Choose from the range of small motifs on pages 96–122.

Variation ideas Use a contrasting colour yarn for the brim.

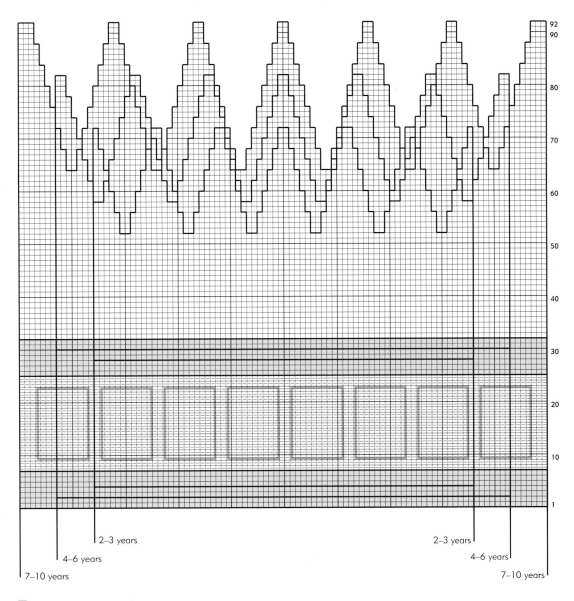

2–3 years

4–6 years

7–10 years

2–3 years

4–6 years

7–10 years

⊟ reverse st st

CHART FOR BRIM OF HAT

For information on:

Edgings   pages 92–95

RIGHT: This hat can be worn with the ties knotted or unknotted. Add tassels or pompons to the ends of the ties for extra character. The ribbed edging can be folded up as shown here or worn down over the ears.

CLASSIC GARMENT
HAT
WITH TIES

To fit 2–3 (4–6, 7–10) years

TO FIT
Ages   2-3 (4-6:7-10) years

YARN
2(3:3) X 50g (1¾oz) balls Rowan Handknit Cotton (photographed in aquamarine); or an equivalent medium weight cotton yarn

NEEDLES AND EXTRAS
1 pair 3.25mm (No10/US 3) needles
1 pair 4mm (No 8/US 6) needles.

TENSION (GAUGE)
20 sts and 28 rows to 10cm (4in) measured over stocking (stockinette) stitch using 4mm (US 6) needles. If necessary, change needles size to obtain correct tension (gauge).

Hat
Cast on 44(56:64) sts using 3.25mm (US 3) needles. Work in K1, P1 rib for 12(17:20) rows.
Change to 4mm (US 6) needles and beg with a K row, work in st st for 28(36:46) rows.
Slip first and last 3 sts onto a safety pin and hold rem sts on a needle.
Work second side to match.
Place RS together and knit together the sts left on the needles.
See page 125 for casting off two edges together.

Making Up
Join side seams.
MAKE TIES
Slip 3 sts held on safety pin from front and 3 sts from back onto one needle and work in K1, P1 rib for 18(25:28)cm/7(9¾:11)in, cast off. Work second tie to match first tie.

HAT
WITH TIES

Ties Work the ties in the same colour and pattern as the hat, or consider using a contrasting colour yarn or stitch pattern (see pages 88–92).

To fit 2–3 (4–6, 7–10) years

Front and back

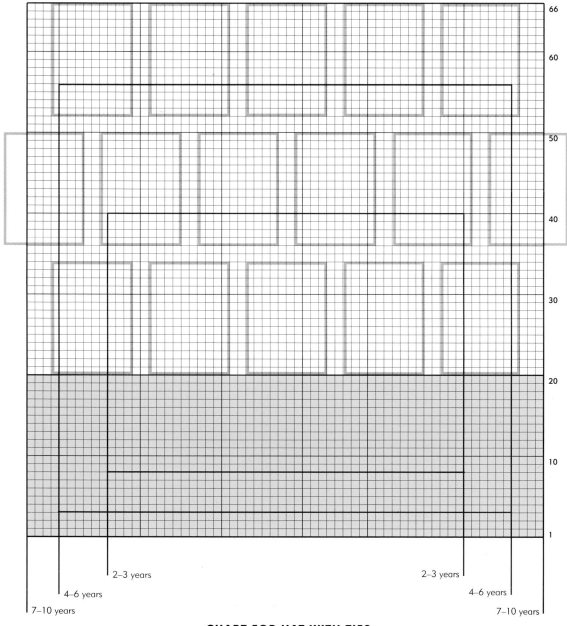

66

60

50

40

30

20

10

1

2–3 years

4–6 years

7–10 years

2–3 years

4–6 years

7–10 years

CHART FOR HAT WITH TIES

Edging Select an edging from the Stitch Library, see pages 92–95. Follow the chart using the depth of the edging as a guide to the start point.

Small motifs These small motifs are perfect for a hat. Choose from the range of small motifs on pages 96–122.

For information on:
Edgings   pages 92–95

69

RIGHT: This bag is ideal for a child to carry for an overnight stay with a friend, or it could be used as a gym or swimming bag. To personalize the bag even further, why not knit in your child's favourite colours.

CLASSIC GARMENT
RUCKSACK
Suitable for ages 2–3 (4–6, 7–10) years

ACTUAL KNITTED MEASUREMENTS

Finished width	25.5(29:32.5)cm/10(11½:12¾)in
Finished Length	27(31:35)cm/10½(12¼:13¾)in

YARN

3(3:4) X 50g (1¾oz) balls of Rowan Handknit Cotton (photographed in blue), or an equivalent medium weight cotton yarn

NEEDLES AND EXTRAS

1 pair 3.25mm (No10/US 3) needles
1 pair 4mm (No 8/US 6) needles.

TENSION (GAUGE)

20 sts and 28 rows to 10cm (4in) measured over stocking (stockinette) stitch using 4mm (US 6) needles. If necessary, change needles size to obtain correct tension (gauge).

Bag

Work 2 pieces as follows;

Cast on 51(58:65) sts using 4mm (US 6) needles.

Work in st st starting with a K row until work measures 23(27:31)cm/ 9(10½:12¼)in, from cast on edge, finishing with a WS row.

Change to 3.25mm (US 3) needles and knit next 6 rows.

NEXT ROW: K4, ▶ yf, K2tog, K5, rep from ▶ to last 5 sts, yo, K2tog, K3.

NEXT ROW: Purl.

Then knit a further 6 rows, cast off.

MAKE STRAP

Take 9 ends of yarn 94(110:126)cm/37(43¼:49½)in long. Plait using 3 lengths of yarn together, (making small balls of yarn with 3 lengths to stop tangling).

Making up

Press all pieces on WS, avoid edging. *See page 125 for pressing.*

Join bottom and side seams using mattress stitch, leaving small hole at bottom of bag to insert strap. *See page 125 for mattress stitch.*

Press seams

Thread cord through eyelets then take each end of strap down to corner of side seam and secure into seam.

For 2–3 (4–6, 7–10) years

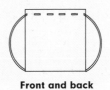

Front and back

Edging Select an edging from the Stitch Library, see pages 92–95. Follow the chart using the depth of the edging as a guide to the start point.

⊡ yarn over

☑ work 2 tog

Medium-sized motifs Choose from the range of medium-sized motifs on pages 96–122.

Small motifs These small motifs are perfect for this bag. Choose from the range of small motifs on pages 96–122.

Strap Work the strap in the same colour and pattern as the main bag, or consider using a contrasting colour yarn or stitch pattern (see pages 88–92).

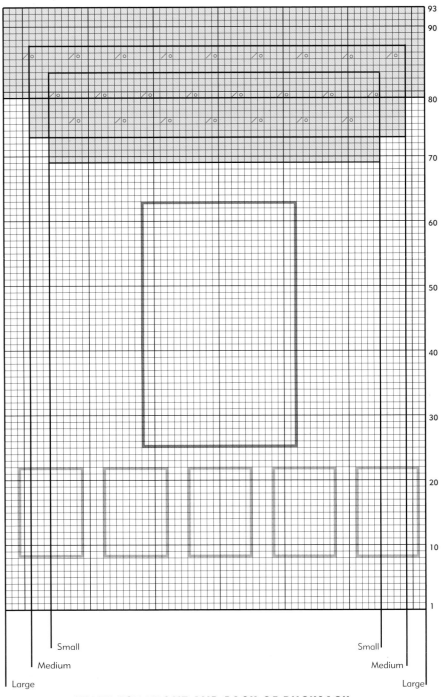

Small

Medium

Large

Small

Medium

Large

CHART FOR FRONT AND BACK OF RUCKSACK

For information on:
Edgings   pages 92–95

RIGHT: Dress this bag up with a fringe for a fashion look, or knit it without a fringe for everyday use. The length of the strap can be shortened or lengthened according to the height of the child.

CLASSIC GARMENT

SQUARE BAG
WITH FRINGE

Suitable for ages 2–3 (4–6, 7–10) years

ACTUAL KNITTED MEASUREMENTS

Finished width	26(29:32)cm/10¼(11½:12½)in
Finished Length	26(29:32)cm/10¼(11½:12½)in

YARN

3(3:4) X 50g (1¾oz) balls of Rowan Handknit Cotton (photographed in red); or an equivalent medium weight cotton yarn

NEEDLES AND EXTRAS

1 pair 3.25mm (No 10/US 3) needles
1 pair 4mm (No 8/US 6) needles.

TENSION (GAUGE)

20 sts and 28 rows to 10cm (4in) measured over stocking (stockinette) stitch using 4mm (US 6) needles. If necessary, change needles size to obtain correct tension (gauge).

Bag

Work 2 pieces as follows;
Cast on 52(58:64) sts using 4mm (US 6) needles.
K8(10:12) rows.
Then work in st st starting with a K row until fabric measures 25.5(28,30.5)cm/10(11:12)in from cast on edge finishing with a RS row

Form hemline

(WS) P1, pick up loop from 6th row down with tip of right needle and place on left needle, purl together with next st, rep across row. ▶▶
Change to 3.25mm (US 3) needles and K8(10:12) rows. Cast off

Make strap as follows;

Cast on 7(8:9) sts and work in garter st until measures 60(65:70)cm/23½(25½,27½)in. Cast off

Making up

Press all pieces on WS, avoid edging. *See page 125 for pressing.*
Join bottom and side seams using mattress stitch. Press seams
Join each end of strap to the centre inside of the side seams.
Add fringe to hemline by taking matching yarn and cut to a length of 28(30:32)cm/11(11¾:12½)in, fold in half to double thread. Draw folded end through hemline, then loose ends through the loop. Pull loose ends firmly to make a knot. Repeat on every stitch. Finish by neatening fringe when complete.

SQUARE BAG
WITH FRINGE

For 2–3 (4–6, 7–10) years

Front and back

work hem

pick up stitches for hem

Hem Add a hem and decorate with a fringe, changing colour to highlight the fringe, see page 83.

Medium-sized motifs Choose from the range of medium-sized motifs on pages 96–122.

Edging Select an edging from the Stitch Library, see pages 92–95. Follow the chart using the depth of the edging as a guide to the start point.

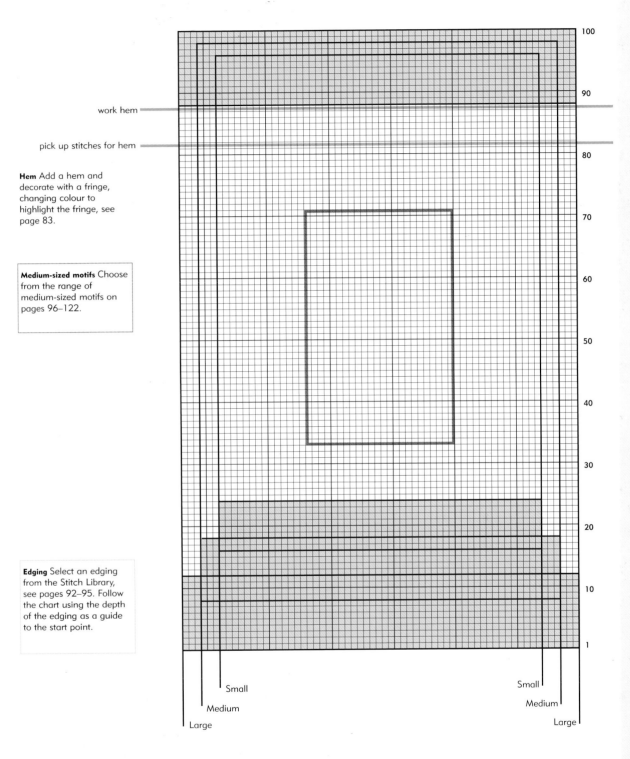

Small
Medium
Large

Small
Medium
Large

CHART FOR FRONT AND BACK OF BAG

For information on:

Edgings   pages 92–95

73

CLASSIC GARMENT PATTERNS
STYLE VARIATIONS

The four basic styles of each pattern can be varied in many different ways. Some of these options are shown in the photographed garments. These variations are explained in detail below and can be added to any of the master patterns. The eight different classic garment sizes have been grouped into three age ranges for these variations as follows: 3 months to 2 years (2 to 6 years, 7 to 10 years). Refer to the correct size for your child's age group or for the pattern you are working. **Note:** Extra yarn will be needed when making certain variations, see below for details.

V-neck pullover necklines

NO BORDER NECKBAND

Follow the instructions for picking up stitches in the master pattern. Beginning with a purl row, work in stocking (stockinette) stitch for 4(6:8) rows or to the required length, ending with a wrong-side row. Cast off loosely. Do not work the shaping at the centre of neck.

K2, P2, RIB NECKBAND

Follow the instructions for picking up stitches in the master pattern. Do not mark the centre st at the front V neck, just mark centre of V. The total number of stitches must be a multiple of 4 stitches plus 2.
ROW 1: ▶ K2, P2, rep from ▶ to last 2 sts, K2. AT THE SAME TIME work to within 2 sts of marked point, work 2 sts tog, work next 2 sts tog, patt to end.
ROW 2: ▶ P2, K2, rep from ▶ to last 2 sts, P2.
Cont in rib as set, at the same time dec as set until band measures 2(3:4)cm/¾(1¼:1½)in.
Cast off loosely in patt.

COWL NECK

Join both shoulder seams.
Using a circular needle, and beginning at the centre of the V neck, pick up the number of stitches stated in the master pattern for right front neck, all the sts across the back neck, and those stated for the left front neck.
Work in a K1, P1 rib or K2, P2 rib backwards and forwards for 2(2.5:3)cm/1¾(1:1¼)in. Cast off loosely in pattern.
Sew one band under the other at the front.

Crewneck pullover necklines

K2, P2 RIB WITH STOCKING STITCH ROLL NECK

This neckband is worked as for K2, P2 rib (see page 93), then with 6(6:8) rows in stocking (stockinette) stitch, starting with a purl row. Cast off loosely in pattern.

CABLED HIGH NECKBAND

You will need 1 extra ball of yarn. This is worked in a cabled border pattern (see page 93) with multiples of 10 stitches plus 2. This cable neckband pulls in considerably, so you need to increase the number of stitches rather than decreasing, to achieve the desired multiple. For example, for the 5–6 years crewneck pullover, 112 stitches are picked up around the neck; this would need to be increased on the first row to 122 stitches.
Repeat these two rows until work measures 4(5:6)cm/1½(2:2½)in or the required length. Cast off loosely in pattern

HIGH NECKBAND WITH ZIP FASTENER

You will need 1 extra ball of yarn. Buy the zip before working this neckband. If you are unable to find a suitable size, cut the zip to fit. This style is recommended only for sizes 4–5 years and upwards. Using a circular needle, and starting and finishing at the centre front, pick up the number of stitches stated in the master pattern. With right side facing, pick up and knit half the stitches on the front spare needle, then the stitches in the right front neck, those across the back, those in the left front neck and the remaining stitches on the spare needle.
Increase/decrease to a multiples of 4 stitches plus 2. Work backwards and forwards in K2, P2 rib.

INDIVIDUAL STYLE: *Choose an alternative collar or neckline to the basic pattern and create your own uniquely-styled pullover or jacket.*

ROW 1: P2, K2 to last 2 sts, P2.

ROW 2: K2, P2, to last 2 sts K2.

Work these 2 rows until neckband measures (8:10)cm/(3:4)in. Then work 3 rows in rev st st.

Cast off loosely in patt.

Sew zip into place using slipstitch.

HOOD

You will need 1(2:2) balls of extra yarn. Using a circular needle, and starting and finishing at the centre front, pick up the number of stitches as stated in the master pattern.

With right side facing, pick up and knit half the number of stitches on the front spare needle, then the stitches in right front neck, those across the back, those in left front neck and the remaining on the spare needle. Work in the round in moss (seed) stitch *(see page 93)* for 6(6:8) rows.

NEXT ROW: Work in moss st AT THE SAME TIME inc one st on every alt st.

Now work backwards and forwards as foll:

Work 3(4:5) sts in moss st, P to last 3(4:5) sts, then work rem sts in moss st.

Cont to work edge sts in moss st and the remainder in st st until the hood measures 14(26:31)cm/5½(10:12)in.

Divide the work in half and place each half on a separate needle. Fold the work with RS facing, and cast sts off together. *For technique see page 125.*

V-neck jacket necklines

K2, P2 RIB WITH STOCKING STITCH ROLL NECK

For this effect, work in K2, P2 rib *(see page 93)* for 4(6:8) rows; then starting with a purl row, work 4(6:8) rows in stocking (stockinette) stitch. Cast off loosely in pattern.

BOX COLLAR

Following the master pattern, work the front bands of the jacket. Then pick up the stitches as stated in the master pattern starting and finishing halfway across the front bands. Therefore, where the pattern states pick up 6 stitches across the top of the right front band you should only pick up 3 stitches.

Suitable stitches for a box collar are moss (seed) stitch, garter stitch or rib *(see pages 92–94).*

Work in your chosen stitch for 8(9:10)cm/3(3½:4)in or to the required depth. Cast off loosely in pattern.

SAILOR COLLAR

You will need 1(2:2) balls of extra yarn. To achieve the best finish, work the front band and collar in moss (seed) stitch *(see page 93).*

First work vertical front bands *(see page 77).*

Left front band and collar

Work band to start of neck shaping finishing with a RS row. Hold sts on needle and slipstitch band into place.

NEXT ROW (WS): Moss 3 sts, K to last st, inc into this last st.

NEXT ROW: P to last 3 sts, moss 3.

Cont as set, inc 1 st every alt row until 14(20:24) sts are on the needle.

Work straight until work fits along front neck to shoulder seam,

ending with a WS row. Hold sts on a needle. Slipstitch into place.
Work second side to match first side rev all shaping.

To complete collar, patt across sts held on first needle, then pick up and knit sts from back as stated in master pattern, down left back neck, on holder at back neck, and up right back neck, finally patt across sts held on second needle.

NEXT ROW: Moss 3 sts, P to last 3 sts, moss 3 sts.

NEXT ROW: Moss 3 sts , K to last 3 sts, moss 3 sts.

Rep last 2 rows until work measures 10(13:18)cms/4(5:7)in.
Work 4 rows in moss st.
Cast off loosely in patt.

LAPELS

You will need 1 extra ball of yarn. To achieve the best finish work the front band and collar in moss (seed) stitch. First work vertical front bands *(see page 77).*

Left front band and collar

Work band to start of neck shaping finishing with a RS row. Hold sts on needle and slipstitch band into place.

NEXT ROW (WS): Moss to last st and inc into this last st.

NEXT ROW: Moss st across row.

Cont as set inc 1 st every alt row at neck edge to 12(16:18) sts.
Work 1 row.

NEXT ROW (RS): Cast off 6(8:10) sts, patt to end.

NEXT ROW: Patt across all sts.

NEXT ROW: Cast on 6(8:10) sts, patt to end.

Cont straight until work fits along front neck across to centre back.
Cast off in patt. Slipstitch into place.

Work second side to match first side, rev all shaping.

Join bands at centre back neck.

Crewneck jacket necklines

COLLAR

You will need 1 extra ball of yarn. Using a circular needle, pick up the number of stitches stated in the master pattern, starting halfway across the right front band, i.e. where the master pattern instructs you to pick up 6 stitches here, you should pick up only 3. Continue to pick up the other stitches as set, finishing halfway across the left front band. Choose from moss (seed) stitch, garter stitch or a rib pattern *(see pages 92–94).*

Work for 8(9:10)cm/3(3½:4)in, or required depth. Cast off loosely in pattern.

HOOD

You will need 1(2:2) balls of extra yarn. With RS facing, pick up and knit the number of stitches stated in the master pattern, starting at the centre front neck. Pick up half of the stitches on the front spare needle, then pick up the stitches in the right front neck, those across the back, those in the left front neck and remaining stitches on the spare needle. Work backwards and forwards in moss (seed) stitch *(see page 93)* for 6(6:8) rows.

NEXT ROW: Work in moss st AT THE SAME TIME inc one st on every alt st.

Work 3(4:5) sts in moss st, P to last 3(4:5) sts, then work rem sts in moss st.

Cont to work edge sts in moss st and the remainder in st st until the hood measures 14(26:31)cm/5½(10:12)in.

Divide the work in half and place each half on a separate needle. Fold the work with RS facing, and cast sts off together. *For technique see page 125.*

Side vents and panels

SIDE VENTS
Work side vents in moss (seed) stitch or garter stitch *(see pages 92–93).*

Work side vents after border has been completed. Change to 4mm (US 6) needles.

ROW 1 (RS): Work the first and last 3(5:7) sts in moss or garter st.

Cont as set for 6(12:18) rows. Then work all sts in st st as stated in basic pattern.

Leave the vents open when sewing up the side seams.

BUTTONED SHOULDER DETAIL

This is shown for the first two sizes.

When adding the button detail, do not work the shoulder shaping.

Left front shoulder

When all neck decreases have been worked, change to moss (seed) stitch *(see page 93)* and work for 2.5cm (1in) AT THE SAME TIME placing buttonholes along the middle row evenly by working (2 sts tog, yo). Complete the right side of front neck normally but without the shoulder shaping.

On the back you should work an extra 2.5cm(1in) in st st on the left shoulder and cast off. Complete Right shoulder normally without shaping the shoulder.

When completing the garment place the buttonhole band on top of the button band and slipstitch tog at armhole edge, then sew in the sleeve.

DECORATIVE DETAIL: It is easy to adapt the basic garment pattern, here we have added a reverse stocking stitch yoke and pocket flaps.

RIBBED SHOULDER DETAIL

When adding this detail, do not work the shoulder shaping.
On both front and back, work the last 4(6:8) rows before the shoulder in K2, P2 rib *(see page 93)*. Mark the number of rows down from the shoulder on the chart. For best results increase stitches to multiples of 4 plus 2, increasing the necessary stitches on the last row of stocking (stockinette) sitcht. Begin with a right-side row. Repeat the last 2 rows for the depth required.

REVERSE STOCKING STITCH YOKE

This is worked half way between the beginning of the armhole and the shoulder shaping. Mark position on chart and work in reverse stocking (stockinette) stitch. If your design doesn't have a shaped armhole, count from the beginning of the V-neck shaping for the jacket.

Fastenings and edgings

ZIP FASTENING

For both Crew- and V-neck jackets

Pick up and knit the front bands as stated in the master pattern, but work them to only half the suggested depth. Sew the zip into place along the centre fronts.

HORIZONTAL BANDS

For a V-neck cardigan

Pick up the number of stitches stated in master pattern from the bottom edge to the beginning of the V-neck shaping. Work in the stitch pattern of your choice.

VERTICAL BANDS

Worked with Sailor collar and Lapels *(see pages 75 and 76)*.

Button band (Make this first.)

Using 3.25mm (US 3) needles cast on 3(5:7) sts and work in moss (seed) stitch) *(see page 93)* as foll:

ROW 1: ▶ K1, P1, rep from ▶ to last st, K1.

ROW 2: As Row 1.

Work until band fits along front edge of cardigan when slightly stretched, slipstitch into place.

Mark position of buttons on band.

Buttonhole band

Work to match button band, working buttonholes to match position of buttons in centre of band.

BUTTONHOLES ROW: Patt to marked position, patt 2 sts tog, yo, patt to end.

TURNED-BACK CUFF WITH BUTTON

You will need 1 extra ball of yarn. Turn up the cuff and sew a button through both thicknesses at the centre of the sleeve seam.

PICOT CAST OFF

This is a very pretty detailing and can be worked on any garter stitch or stocking (stockinette) stitch collar or neckband.

Work the collar or neck edging of your choice, decreasing if necessary to a multiple of 3 stitches plus 2 on the first row of the collar or neckband. *See Picot cast off on page 93.*

Pockets

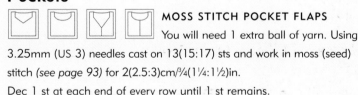

MOSS STITCH POCKET FLAPS

You will need 1 extra ball of yarn. Using 3.25mm (US 3) needles cast on 13(15:17) sts and work in moss (seed) stitch *(see page 93)* for 2(2.5:3)cm/¾(1¼:1½)in.

Dec 1 st at each end of every row until 1 st remains.

Fasten off.

PATCH POCKETS

A patch pocket can be placed on the front of the garment or on a sleeve. You will need 1 extra ball of yarn. Using 4 mm needles cast on 12(14:20) sts. Beg with a K row work 7(8:11)cm/2¾(1:1¼)in in st st. Change to 3.25mm (US 3) needles and work in chosen edging st patt to match borders and cuffs for 1(2:2.5)cm/½(¾:1)in. Cast off. Slipstitch into place.

Creative Library

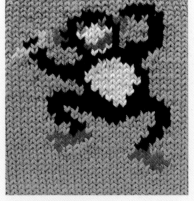

This chapter provides you with the ideas and techniques you will need to personalize your child's garment. Let the child pick out their a motif from the huge selection in the motif library. Together select an edging or border that will make the garment fun and unique. Create your own motif design for the child, using a favourite animal, toy or hero. In an easy step-by-step format, you will be shown how to do this in the following pages.

Also included is help on picking and mixing colours, on introducing texture into the fabric and on combining motifs. Tips on working with pattern repeats are provided, as well as a section covering all the knitting techniques you will need, from working with more than one colour to sewing up your garment.

Inspiration by design

This chapter gives you all the help you will need to create your own garment without having to be a professional designer. Do not be daunted by the idea of designing a garment, all the elements are here, laid out in an easy-to-follow format and clear language. We have tried to demystify the process of designing by ensuring that all the garments selected are simple; motifs are there for you to mix and match in any way you like. If you want to design your own motifs, a good starting point is to look around your immediate environment for inspiration; look at everyday things, familiar places such as your garden, or base a drawing on a trip to the seaside, a day out at the zoo or the circus. You could start with an object as simple as a child's toy on which you can base a design. To get you started see page 84.

Working with more than one colour

Mixing colours in a garment can seem a little daunting, but with a few basic guidelines you will feel confident enough to change and mix colours.

You can select colours to create different moods, to follow fashion trends and to suit different personalities. Generally speaking, green is a calm colour, blue is a cool colour, red is a passionate colour, yellow is a warm colour and cream is a soothing colour.

Mixing complimentary colours – that is, colours that sit opposite each other on the colour wheel – will give you the most contrast and a bold design. Examples of this are orange and blue or turquoise and red. For less contrast and a smoothly blended effect, mix colours that sit next to each other on the colour wheel, such as blue and purple or red and orange.

SWATCH BELOW

MIXING COLOURS *A colour looks quite different depending on the colours it is placed next to. Look at the patterned swatch below and study the variations. Follow the orange band from the bottom left-hand corner of the page upwards. See how vibrant it is against the green and blue and how it seems to come forward. By contrast, against the dark pink and red it recedes into the background, almost disappearing.*

When only a small amount of a colour is used in a motif, such as for a mouth, make sure that the colour chosen for the background allows the few stitches to show up. A few stitches of bright orange for a chick's beak against a cream background will bring the chicks alive.

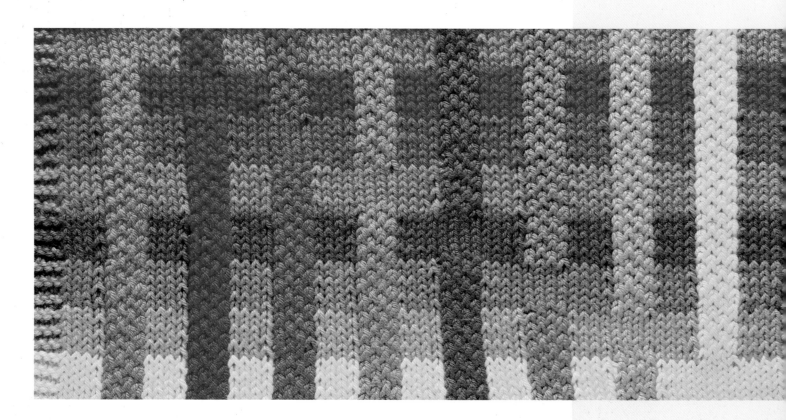

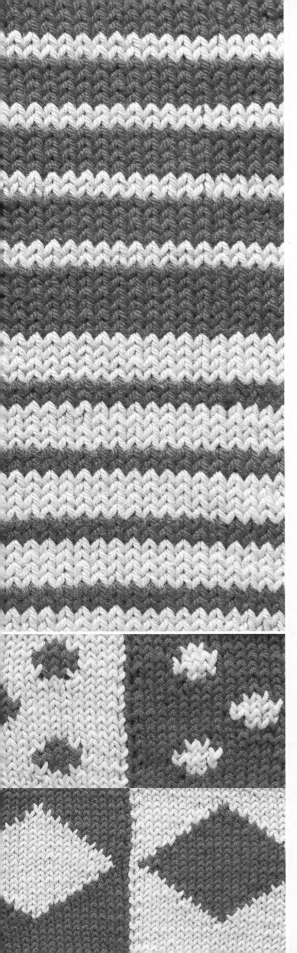

SWATCHES ON LEFT

PROPORTION OF COLOURS *If you knit horizontal stripes in two contrasting colours the relative size of the dominant colour (in this case the red) determines the vibrancy of your design. Increase the pink and you will see that the design becomes softer and less dramatic.*

SPOTS AND BLOCKS OF COLOUR

Look how the design changes by simply reversing the colours. The red triangle and red spots come forward and are dominant. In contrast, the pink triangle and spots recede and are softer, as if they are leading your eye through the shape.

SWATCHES ON RIGHT

BRIGHT OR NEUTRAL? *Vivid colours are ideal for children's knitting and work perfectly when mixed together to create an eye-catching design. Mix orange, green and yellow on a turquoise background for a summery combination. However, if you prefer neutrals, use natural or earth colours together to create harmony and a classic look. These colours are easier to mix and match with other items of clothing, making your design less vulnerable to changing colour fashions.*

MIXING COLOUR TONES *Deeper tones are heavier and seem to come forward, while paler colours are lighter and appear to recede. Mix light tones together for a softer look; dark and light tones together for bold contrast; and darker tones together for a richer design.*

CHANGING COLOURS *On both colourways, the buttons and trim of the bear's jacket are harmonious, whereas the yellow of the bear's body is a bold contrast against the background, making it stand out from the background.*

81

When choosing colours for the motifs and backgrounds, place a ball of each colour together and see what effect they have on one another. Next, work a sample, placing the colours as they will be combined in the garment. Choose your background colour carefully, and decide whether your motifs will show up on this colour. Half close your eyes and you will be able to see if there is enough contrast. If you wish to create a patchwork effect in the garment, place the motifs on different-coloured backgrounds.

Edgings

The edging you choose will frame and complete the look of your garment. For a seaside theme, pick a zigzag edging to suggest waves. Turn a jacket into a special party outfit by adding a frill to the cast-on edge, or a leafy edging to complement flower motifs.

An edging or border can be worked in two different ways. You can either begin it immediately after casting on, so that it is knitted vertically along with the main fabric, or you can knit a separate border or edging horizontally and then sew it on. The way you work will be determined by the edging you choose, which can range from a simple garter-stitch band to a more complicated lacy edging. You can use the same edging on the sleeves and the front and back of the garment, or you can choose different edgings that complement each other.

LEFT: *Edgings can completely change the look of a garment. They can be worked at the beginning of the knitting process or added after the garment is finished.*

WORKING WITH REPEAT PATTERNS

To work a repeated pattern, you must first work out how many stitches and rows you have to the pattern repeat. On a textured or lace pattern that has written instructions, the repeat is the number of stitches between the ▶▶. When working from a chart, look to see where the repeat starts and finishes, and mark with a coloured line. Then divide the number of stitches in the piece of knitting by the number of stitches in the repeat to get the number of repeats that you will need to work across the row. The number may not be exact and you may have a few stitches left over. Balance the repeats by placing half of these extra stitches at the beginning and half at the end of the row.

Some of the lace and textured patterns refer to multiples of stitches; this is another way of giving the number of stitches in a pattern repeat.

WAVE DESIGN *These waves have a ten-stitch pattern repeat. If your border was 122 stitches wide then you could work the pattern of ten stitches twelve times, but you would have two stitches left over. So, to knit a balanced border, you would need to add one extra stitch at the beginning and end of the row.*

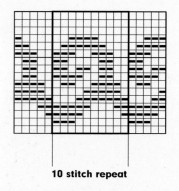

10 stitch repeat

SWATCHES ON LEFT

MOSS (SEED) STITCH EDGING *By casting on using a contrasting yarn and working one row before changing to the main colour, you can add a trim.*

GARTER-STITCH EDGING *Create a bold line by casting on with a contrasting colour when working a garter stitch border.*

GARTER-STITCH EDGING WITH BLANKET-STITCH EMBROIDERY *Decorate an edging by embroidering it with blanket stitch in a contrasting yarn for extra interest.*

RIB WITH A CURLED EDGE *Give the garment an up-to-date fashion look by working four rows in stocking (stockinette) stitch in a contrasting colour, then changing it to the rib pattern.*

TWO-COLOURED RIB *Stripe a K2, P2 rib by working with two colours. See page 92 for rib pattern.*

EYELET PATTERN WITH RIBBON *Thread a ribbon in a contrasting colour through the holes of the eyelet pattern to dress up this simple edging. See page 94 for eyelet pattern.*

SWATCHES ON RIGHT

DOUBLE-FRILL EDGING *Work two frill edgings in contrasting colours, one shorter than the other, and join by knitting them together from the needles. See page 93 for frill pattern.*

FRINGE *Add fringe to a jacket by cutting lengths of yarn and looping these through every stitch of the cast-on edge with a crochet hook. Work the fringe in either the same colour as the garment or in a contrasting colour.*

HEM WITH FRINGE *Create a cowboy look by adding a fringe to the yoke of a jacket or to a bag. Working the yoke in a colour contrasting with the rest of the garment creates a hem at base of the yoke by picking up loops of the stitches four rows below, and working them together with the stitches on the needle. Then loop lengths through the hem to form the fringe.*

Some edgings can be worked only to a given depth, whereas others may be worked to any measurement desired. Working the edging in a different colour from that of the main knitting will add contrast. Integrate the contrasting edging by choosing a colour that has been used in the motifs on the garment.

Motifs

In the Motif library (*see pages 96–122*) there are three different sizes of motifs, along with some simple Fair Isle borders. The small motifs measure 5cm (2in) square and are worked over 10 stitches and 14 rows. The medium-sized motifs measure 12cm (4¾in) square and are worked over 24 stitches and 34 rows. The large motifs measure 25cm (10in) square and are worked over 50 stitches and 70 rows. Lastly, the Fair Isle borders are all repeats of 10 stitches over 14 rows. All the motifs are centred in their given square; some fit edge to edge and some have space around them.

The motifs have been grouped by theme, such as farmyard or seaside, but motifs can be combined to create your own theme. Have fun choosing and placing motifs. There are lots of different combinations and areas where you can place your motif. On the master garment chart there is a guide to where the three different size motifs can be placed. However, these are only suggestions; do your own thing and place your motifs wherever you like. Watch out for the necklines and armholes; place the motifs away from these shaping points.

Changing the look of a motif is simply done by changing the colour used. Knit the motifs in pretty pastel shades for a baby or in bold, bright primary colours for an older child. Mix different scales of motif together to create a picture. For example, use a large skeleton motif in the centre of a pullover, edge the back and front with a small skull and crossbones design; and pattern the sleeves with stripes of the same design in alternating colours. Or keep the garment very simple by just adding a small motif to a patch pocket, or one large motif to the centre, or a little border to the bottom of the front, back and sleeves. You can also customize a child's bag or hat by adding a large motif in the centre of a bag or a small motif on the rim of a hat.

RIGHT: *A clown's head motif will give a party look to any toddlers garment.*

CREATE YOUR OWN MOTIF

First decide upon the theme of your motif and how big you wish it to be. Change the measurements of your motif into squares by using the tension (gauge) of the knitting. For example, to create a motif that is 10cm (4in) square, you multiply 10cm (4in) by the stitch tension (gauge) of 2 stitches/cm (5 stitches/in) and also by the row tension (gauge) of 2.8 stitches/cm (7 stitches/in), which gives you 20 stitches and 28 rows in the motif. Draw a box to this size on graph paper, and sketch your image on the grid. Next, square off the curves and diagonals to create a full squared outline. If the curves cut across more than half a square step the square up and if it cuts through less than half take it down. Then fill in the outlined shapes with colour.

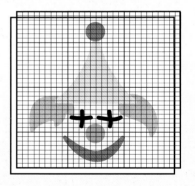

Note Stitches are wider than they are tall. So if you draw an image on ordinary graph paper exactly the shape you want it, the knitted version will be slightly flattened. Therefore, either design on specially proportioned graph paper or make your motif slightly longer and thinner to compensate. It will revert back to realistic proportions once it is knitted.

SWATCHES ON LEFT

DIFFERENT-COLOURED FISH

Here, the use of different colours for the fish creates the impression that some of the fish are nearer to you and others are farther away.

CHANGING PATTERNS *Changing the coloured patterns on the fish and their backgrounds adds an extra dimension to the design and its characterization.*

FISH SCALES *Mixing different sizes of fish creates a 3-D effect and the illusion of movement within the design. Also, by edging the main part of your design with a border of smaller fish on a darker background, you are creating a frame around the central image through which depth of field is suggested.*

SWATCHES ON RIGHT

STRIPES *Stripes can be produced using the same Fair Isle repeat but changing the background colour. This is suitable for patterning sleeves or an entire garment.*

CHEQUERED EFFECT *Create a chequerboard effect by using the same two colours alternately for background and for motif. This can be worked using any of the medium-size or small motifs.*

BORDER PATTERNS *Use a small heart motif horizontally to edge the bottom of a jacket and vertically to frame the front opening. Worked with a large-scale heart in the centre of the front panels the jacket is complete.*

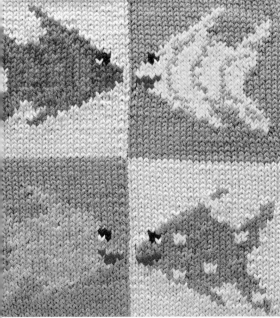

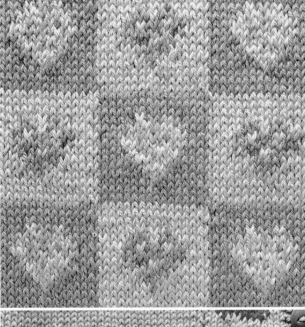

SWATCHES ON LEFT

BEACH BALL *Work the beach ball shape with alternate coloured stripes and reverse stocking (stockinette) stitch on a border.*

WAVES *Instead of working the pattern of the wave in a contrasting colour, work it in stocking (stockinette) stitch on a reverse stocking (stockinette) stitch background.*

APPLE TREE *Make the apples three-dimensional on the tree by working the one red stitch into a bobble.*

SHEEPDOG *Give the sheepdog a shaggy tactile tummy by working the stitches in moss (seed) stitch.*

SWATCHES ON RIGHT

PARROT *Create a chequerboard effect without changing the background colour. This is done by alternating squares of moss (seed) stitch with the parrot motif, which sits on a background of stocking (stockinette) stitch. Changing the direction of the motifs adds extra interest.*

CAT AND MOUSE *Combine a cat and mouse on the same background and add a square grid of reverse stocking (stockinette) stitch. The grid is worked over 2 stitches and 2 rows.*

FLOWERS *Alternate a coloured flower on a stocking (stockinette)stitch background with a textured flower on a reverse stocking (stockinette) stitch background.*

ADDING TEXTURE TO THE MOTIFS

Working shapes in a contrasting texture instead of a different colour will add depth to the knitted fabric by making it more tactile and sculptural. Remember that texture can be achieved quite simply by placing one stitch pattern next to another. For example squares of reverse stocking (stockinette) stitch sitting next to squares of stocking stitch will produce a chequerboard effect.

Plot the textures you are going to work as if they were coloured shapes or lines. You can add a textured grid to the fabric, using this to frame the main motif or multiples of smaller motifs. If you wish to exaggerate the three-dimensional quality of your design, try adding bobbles to help it. An example of this would be to use bobbles as a flower head or as defining an apple in a tree. Finally, you might add texture to highlight the special characteristics of a favourite animal, such as the ruff on a dog's chest, the shell of a tortoise or the mane of a roaring lion.

Designing your own garments

Now that you have explored all the different elements for creating your own garment, you can get started on combining motifs, colours and edgings on a garment pattern to create your own special designs.

Here is an example of how you can transform a plain basic garment with a round neck into a seaside theme.

TROPICAL FISH PULLOVER

Centre the tropical fish motif (*see page 111*) on the front of the pullover. Edge the bottom of the front, back and sleeves with a wave strip border (*see page 98*), picking out the pink stripe on one of the angel fish to use as the background colour of the wave. Work the wave in the same colour as the background fabric to balance the design. Edge the front and back with a garter-stitch zigzag edging (*see page 93*) in a contrasting colour to suggest the cliffs on a seashore. Work the neckband and cuffs in garter stitch to match the texture on the zigzag edging. Finally, add interest to the sleeves by adding a starfish motif (*see page 109*) with a different-coloured background to create a patchwork effect.

BELOW: *Choose a theme to match your child's interests. If your child loves the seaside then they will love this combinations of motifs and edging.*

Stitch library

The Stitch library is full of different ideas to enhance your knitted fabric and bring an individual signature to your chosen design. These include a wide range of different edgings and borders and a large selection of lace and textured patterns which will give your work a more three-dimensional quality. You can also add textural quality to your knitting by choosing a knit and purl combination or a bobble or heart cable. It is important to remember, however, that textured work must not be pressed directly by a hot iron, as this will flatten the stitch pattern, instead, hold a steam iron slightly above the fabric and steam gently *(see page 125 for advice on pressing).*

Knit and purl combinations

Simply by combining knit and purl stitches in different ways, you can create many different fabrics. These can be used for the main fabric or for contrasts in a specific area. For example, you could use the hortizonial or vertical repeat of a pattern to create stripes. By using a different colour for the textured stitch, you could add an extra dimension. *(See 'Working with repeat patterns', page 82)*

STOCKING (STOCKINETTE) STITCH CIRCLES

Work with a multiple of 10 sts + 1.

ROW 1 (RS): Purl.
ROW 2: Knit.
ROW 3: P4, ▶ K3, P7, rep from ▶ to last 7 sts, K3, P4.
ROW 4: K3, ▶ P5, K5, rep from ▶ to last 8 sts, P5, K3.
ROWS 5 & 7: P2, ▶ K7, P3, rep from ▶ to last 9 sts, K7, P2.
ROWS 6 & 8: K2, ▶ P7, K3, rep from ▶ to last 9 sts, P7, K2.
ROW 9: P3, ▶ K5, P5, rep from ▶ to last 8sts, K5, P3.
ROW 10: K4, ▶ P3, K7, rep from ▶ to last 7 sts, P3, K4.
ROW 11: Purl.
ROW 12: Knit.

ROW 13: K2, ▶ P7, K3, rep from ▶ to last 9 sts, P7, K2.
ROW 14: P3, ▶ K5, P5, rep from ▶ to last 8 sts, K5, P3.
ROWS 15 & 17: K4, ▶ P3, K7, rep from ▶ to last 7 sts, P3, K4.
ROWS 16 & 18: P4, ▶ K3, P7, rep from ▶ to last 7 sts, K3, P4.
ROW 19: K3, ▶ P5, K5, rep from ▶ to last 8 sts, P5, K3.
ROW 20: P2, ▶ K7, P3, rep from ▶ to last 9 sts, K7, P2.
These 20 rows form the repeat.

GARTER STITCH LINES

Work with a multiple of 10 sts.

ROW 1 (RS): K2, ▶ P6, K4, rep from ▶ to last 8 sts, P6, K2.
ROW 2 & EVERY ALT ROW: Purl.

ROW 3: Knit.
ROW 5: P3, ▶ K4, P6, rep from ▶ to last 7 sts, K4, P3.
ROW 7: Knit.
ROW 8: Purl.
These 8 rows form the repeat.

SQUARE GRIDS

Work with a multiple of 10 sts.

ROW 1 (RS): K4, ▶ P2, K8, rep from ▶ to last 6 sts, P2, K4.
ROW 2: P4, ▶ K2, P8, rep from ▶ to last 6 sts, K2, P4.
Rep these 2 rows 4 times.
ROW 11: Purl.
ROW 12: Knit.
These 12 rows form the repeat.

CHECKERBOARD

Work a with multiple of 20 sts.

ROW 1 (RS): ▶ P10, K10, rep from ▶ to end.
Rep this row 11 more times.
ROW 13: ▶ K10, P10, rep from ▶ to end.
Rep this row 11 more times.
These 24 rows form the repeat.

CROSSES

Work with a multiple of 15 sts on a background of st st.

ROW 1 (RS): K2, ▶ P3, K4, P3, K5, rep from ▶ to last 13 sts, P3, K4, P3, K3.
ROW 2: P4, ▶ K3, P2, K3, P7, rep from ▶ to last 11 sts, K3, P2, K3, P3.
ROW 3: K4, ▶ P6, K9, rep from ▶ to last 11 sts, P6, K5.
ROW 4: P6, ▶ K4, P11, rep from ▶ to last 9 sts, K4, P5.
ROW 5: K6, ▶ P2, K13, rep from ▶ to last 9 sts, P2, K7.
ROW 6: P7, ▶ K2, P13, rep from ▶ to last 8 sts, K2, P6.

ROW 7: K5, ▶ P4, K11, rep from ▶ to last 10 sts, P4, K6.

ROW 8: P5, ▶ K6, P9, rep from ▶ to last 10 sts, K6, P4.

ROW 9: K3, ▶ P3, K2, P3, K7, rep from ▶ to last 12 sts, P3, K2, P3, K4.

ROW 10: P3, ▶ K3, P4, K3, K5, rep from ▶ to last 12 sts, K3, P4, K3, P2.

ROW 11: Knit.

ROW 12: Purl.

ROW 13: Knit.

ROW 14: Purl.

These 14 rows form the repeat.

GARTER STITCH DIAMONDS

Work with a multiple of 10 sts + 1.

ROW 1 (RS): Knit.

ROW 2 & EVERY ALT ROW: Purl.

ROWS 3 & 19: K5, ▶ P1, K9, rep from ▶ to last 6 sts, P1, K5.

ROWS 5 & 17: K4, ▶ P3, K7, rep from ▶ to last 7 sts, P3, K4.

ROWS 7 & 15: K3, ▶ P5, K5, rep from ▶ to last 8 sts, P5, K3.

ROWS 9 & 13: K2, ▶ P7, K3, rep from ▶ to last 9 sts, P7, K2.

ROW 11: K1, ▶ P9, K1, rep from ▶ to end.

ROW 20: Purl.

These 20 rows form the repeat.

Lace

Lace patterns can be used in various ways – for the overall fabric or in vertical or horizontal panels. A lace pattern gives knitting a more feminine look. A lace panel can be inserted vertically between motifs or horizontally, alternating with a Fair Isle border. (*See 'Working with repeat patterns', page 82.*)

Overall lace

TEARDROPS

Work with a multiple of 6 sts.

ROW 1 (RS): P4, yo, P2tog, rep from ▶ to end.

ROWS 2, 4 & 6: K1, ▶ P1, K5, rep from ▶ to last 5 sts, P1, K4.

ROWS 3 & 5: P4, ▶ K1, P5, rep from ▶ to last 2 sts, K1, P1.

ROW 7: P1, ▶ yo, P2tog, P4, rep from ▶ to last 5 sts, yo, P2tog, P3.

ROWS 8, 10 & 12: K4, ▶ P1, K5, rep from ▶ to last 2 sts, P1, K1.

ROWS 9 & 11: P1, ▶ K1, P5, rep from ▶ to last 5 sts, K1, P4.

These 12 rows form the repeat.

BOXY EYELETS

Work with a multiple of 10 sts + 5.

ROW 1 (RS): Knit.

ROW 2: Purl.

ROW 3: K1, P3, ▶ K7, P3, rep from ▶ to last st, K1.

ROW 4: P1, K3, ▶ P7, K3, rep from ▶ to last st, P1.

ROW 5: K1, yo, K3tog, yo, ▶ K7, yo, K3tog, yo, rep from ▶ to last st, K1.

ROW 6: Purl.

ROW 7: Knit.

ROW 8: Purl.

ROW 9: K6, ▶ P3, K7, rep from ▶ to last 9 sts, P3, K6.

ROW 10: P6, ▶ K3, P7, rep from ▶ to last 9 sts, K3, P6.

ROW 11: K6, ▶ yo, K3tog, yo, K7, rep from ▶ to last 9 sts, yo, K3tog, yo, K6.

ROW 12: Purl.

These 12 rows form the repeat.

PAIRS OF EYELETS

Work with a multiple of 10 sts + 1.

ROW 1 (RS): Knit.

ROW 2 & EVERY ALT ROW: Purl.

ROW 3: K3, ▶ K2tog, yo, K1, yo, sl1 K1 psso, K5, rep from ▶ to last 8 sts, K2tog, yo, K1, yo, sl1 K1 psso, K3.

ROW 5: Knit

ROW 7: K1, ▶ yo, sl1 K1 psso, K5, K2tog, yo, K1, rep from ▶ to end.

ROW 8: Purl.

These 8 rows form the repeat.

Vertical lace panels

RIGHT-TWIST BRAIDS

Panel of 7 sts on a background of st st.

ROW 1 & EVERY ALT ROW (WS): Purl.

ROW 2: K2, K2tog, yo, K3.

ROW 4: K1, K2tog, yo, K1, yo, sl1 K1 psso, K1.

ROW 6: K2tog, yo, K3, yo, sl1 K1 psso.

ROW 8: K2tog, yo, K2, K2tog, yo, K1.

ROW 10: K2, yo, K3tog, yo, K2.

These 10 rows form the repeat.

LEFT-TWIST BRAIDS

Panel of 7sts on background of st st.

ROW 1 & EVERY ALT ROW (WS): Purl.

ROW 2: K3, yo, sl1 K1 psso, K2.

ROW 4: K1, K2tog, yo, K1, yo, sl1 K1 psso, K1.

ROW 6: K2tog, yo, K3, yo, sl1 K1 psso.

ROW 8: K1, yo, sl1 K1 psso, K2, yo, sl1 K1 psso.

ROW 10: K2, yo, sl1, K2tog, psso, yo, K2.

These 10 rows form the repeat.

DIAGONAL EYELETS PANEL

Panel of 6 sts on a background of st st.

ROW 1: K1, yo, sl1 K1 psso, K1, yo, sl1 K1 psso.

ROW 2 & EVERY ALT ROW: Purl.

ROW 3: K2, yo, sl1 K1 psso, K2.

ROW 5: K3, yo, sl1 K1 psso, K1.

ROW 6: Purl.

These 6 rows form the repeat.

Horizontal lace borders

LACY DIAMONDS BORDER

Work with a multiple of 8 sts, on a background of st st.

ROW 1 (RS): K3, ▶ yo, sl1 K1 psso, K6, rep from ▶ to last 5 sts, yo, sl1 K1 psso, K3.

ROW 2 & EVERY ALT ROW: Purl.

ROW 3: K2, ▶ (yo, sl1 K1 psso) twice, K4, rep from ▶ to last 6 sts, (yo, sl1 K1 psso) twice, K2.

ROW 5: K1, ▶ (yo, sl1 K1 psso) 3 times, K2, rep from ▶ to last 7 sts, (yo, sl1 K1 psso) 3 times, K1.

ROW 7: As row 3.

ROW 9: As row 1.

ROW 10: Purl.

LITTLE WHEEL PANEL

Work with a multiple of 7 sts on a background of st st.

ROW 1 (RS): ▶ K1, K2tog, yo, K1, yo, sl1 K1 psso, K1, rep from ▶ to end.

ROW 2: ▶ P2togb, yo, P3, yo, P2tog, rep from ▶ to end.

ROW 3: ▶ K1, yo, K2tog, yo, sl1, K2tog, psso, yo, K1, rep from ▶ to end

ROW 4: ▶ P1, yo, P2tog, P1, P2togb, yo, P1, rep from ▶ to end.

ROW 5: ▶ K2, yo, sl1, K2tog, psso, yo, K2, rep from ▶ to end.

ROW 6: Purl.

ZIGZAG PANEL

Work with a multiple of 8 sts + 1 on a background of st st.

ROW 1 (RS): Purl.

ROW 2: Purl.

ROW 3: ▶ K1, yo, sl1 K1 psso, K3, K2tog, yo ▶, rep from ▶ to last st, K1.

ROW 4: Purl.

ROW 5: ▶ K2, yo, sl1 K1 psso, K1, K2tog, yo, K1 ▶ rep from ▶ to last st, K1.

ROW 6: Purl.

ROW 7: ▶ K3, yo, sl1, K2tog, psso, yo, K2 ▶, K1.

ROW 8: Knit.

Cables, Twists and Crosses

You can add a three-dimensional quality to your knitting by introducing cables, twists and crosses These may pull the fabric in a little, so make sure you balance the patterns evenly across the garment or add a few extra stitches when you cast on to compensate for this.

EYES

Work with a multiple of 16 sts + 10.

ROW 1 (RS): Knit.

ROW 2 & EVERY ALT ROWS: Purl.

ROWS 3, 7, 11 & 15: Knit.

ROW 5: K9, C4B, C4F, ▶ K8, C4B, C4F, rep from ▶ to last 9 sts, K9.

ROW 9: K9, C4F, C4B, ▶ K8, C4F, C4B, rep from ▶ to last 9 sts, K9.

ROW 13: K1, C4B, C4F, ▶ K8, C4B, C4F, rep from ▶ to last st, K1.

ROW 17: K1, C4F, C4B, ▶ K8, C4F, C4B, rep from ▶ to last st, K1.

ROW 18: Purl.

These 18 rows form the repeat.

FLYING BIRDS

Work with a multiple of 10 sts + 8.

ROW 1 (RS): Knit.

ROW 2: Purl.

ROW 3: K8, ▶ sl2 purlwise, K8, rep from ▶ to end.

ROW 4: P8, ▶ sl2 purlwise, P8, rep from ▶ to end.

ROW 5: K6, ▶ C3B, C3F, K4, rep from ▶ to end.

ROWS 6 & 8: Purl.

ROW 7: Knit.

ROW 9: K3, ▶ sl2 purlwise, K8, rep from to last 5 sts ▶ sl2 purlwise, K3.

ROW 10: P3, ▶ sl2 purlwise, P8, rep from to last 5 sts ▶ sl2 purlwise, P3.

ROW 11: K1, ▶ C3B, C3F, K4, rep from ▶ to last 7 sts, C3B, C3F, K1.

ROW 12: Purl.

These 12 rows form the repeat.

HEART

Work with a multiple of 15 sts + 3.

ROW 1 (RS): Purl.

ROW 2: Knit.

ROW 3: P8, ▶ K2, P13, rep from ▶ to last 10 sts, K2, P8.

ROW 4: K8, ▶ P2, K13, rep from ▶ to last 10 sts, P2, K8.

ROW 5: P7, ▶ T2B, T2F, P11, rep from ▶ to last 11 sts, T2B, T2F, P7.

ROW 6: K7, ▶ P4, K11, rep from ▶ to last 11 sts, P4, K7.

ROW 7: P6, ▶ T3B, T3F, P9, rep from ▶ to last 12 sts, T3B, T3F, P6.

ROW 8: K6, ▶ P2, K2, P2, K9, rep from ▶ to last 12 sts, P2, K2, P2, K6.

ROW 9: P5, ▶ T3B, P2, T3F, P7, rep from ▶ to last 13 sts, T3B, P2, T3F, P5.

ROW 10: K5, ▶ P2, K4, P2, K7, rep from ▶ to last 13 sts, P2, K4, P2, K5.

ROW 11: P4, ▶ T3B, P4, T3F, P5, rep from ▶ to last 14 sts, T3B, P4, T3F, P4.

ROW 12: K4, ▶ P2, K6, P2, K5, rep from ▶ to last 14 sts, P2, K6, P2, K4.

ROW 13: P3, ▶ T3B, P6, T3F, P3, rep from ▶ to end.

ROWS 14,16 & 18: K3, ▶ P2, K8, P2, K3, rep from ▶ to end.

ROWS 15 & 17: P3, ▶ K2, P8, K2, P3, rep from ▶ to end.

ROW 19: P3, ▶ T3F, P2, K2, P2, T3B, P3, rep from ▶ to end.

ROW 20: K4, ▶ P2, K2, P2, K2, P2, K5, rep from ▶ to last 14 sts, P2, K2, P2, K2, P2, K4.

ROW 21: P4, ▶ T3F, T2B, T2F, T3B, P5, rep from ▶ to last 14 sts, T3F, T3B, T3F, T3B, P4.

ROW 22: K5, ▶ P3, K2, P3, K7, rep from ▶ to last 13 sts, P3, K2, P3, K5.

ROW 23: Purl.

ROW 24: Knit.

PEANUT PATTERN

Work with a multiple of 6 sts + 5.

ROW 1 (RS): Purl.

ROW 2: Knit.

ROW 3: P5, ▶ (K1, P1, K1) all into next st, P5, rep from ▶ to end.

ROWS 4, 6 & 8: K5, ▶ P3, K5, rep from ▶ to end.

ROWS 5 & 7: P5, ▶ K3, P5, rep from ▶ to end.

ROW 9: P5, ▶ K3togb, P5, rep from ▶ to end.

ROW 10: Knit.

ROWS 11 & 13: Purl.

ROW 12 & 14: Knit.

ROW 13: P2, ▶ (K1, P1, K) all into next st, P5, rep from ▶ to last 3 sts (K1, P1, K) all into next st, P2.

ROWS 14, 16 & 18: K2, ▶ P3, K5, rep from ▶ to last 5 sts, P3, K2.

ROWS 15 & 17: P2, ▶ K3, P5, rep from ▶ to last 5 sts, K3, P2.

ROW 19: P2, ▶ K3togb, P5, rep from ▶ to last 5 sts, K3togb, P2.

ROWS 20, 22 & 24: Knit.

ROWS 21 & 23: Purl.

These 24 rows form the repeat.

Bobbles

Bobbles can be fun to add to a plain fabric or to enhance a motif. Work them in a different colour to create flower heads, or in a cluster for the centre of a pattern. (See 'Working with repeat patterns' page 82.)

ROW OF LITTLE FLOWERS

Work with a multiple of 10 sts + 3 on a background of st st.

ROWS 1 & 3 (RS): Using pale yellow yarn, knit.

ROWS 2 & 4: Purl.

ROW 5: Using green yarn, knit.

ROW 6: K5, ▶ K3 wrapping yarn 3 times around needle for each st, K7, rep from ▶ to last 8 sts, K3 wrapping yarn 3 times around needle for each st, K5.

ROW 7: Using pale yellow yarn, K1, ▶ sl1, K3, sl3 dropping extra loops, K3, rep from ▶ to last 2 sts, sl1, K1.

ROW 8: P1, ▶ sl1, P3, sl3, P3, rep from ▶ to last 2 sts, sl1, P1.

ROW 9: K5, ▶ sl3, K7, rep from ▶ to last 8 sts, sl3, K5.

ROW 10: P5, ▶ sl3, P7, rep from ▶ to last 8 sts, sl3, P5.

ROW 11: K3, ▶ sl2, drop next st off needle to front of work, sl the same 2 sts back on to left-hand needle, pick up dropped st and K it; K3, drop next st off needle to front of work, K2, pick up

dropped st and K it; K3, rep from ▶ to end.

ROW 12: Using pink yarn, P1, sl2 ▶ (P1, K1, P1 into next st, sl2) twice, P1, K1, P1 into next st, sl3 rep from ▶ to last 10 sts, (P1, K1, P1 into next st, sl2) 3 times, P1.

ROW 13: K1, sl2, ▶ make bobble (MB) in next 3 sts as foll: yf, P3, turn and K3, turn and sl1, K2tog, psso to complete bobble, (sl2, MB) twice, sl3, rep from ▶ to last 10 sts (MB, sl2) 3 times, K1.

ROW 14: Using pale yellow, purl the row, purling into the back of each bobble.

ROW 15: Knit.

ROW 16: Purl.

DIAMONDS WITH CLUSTER OF BOBBLES

Work with a multiple of 10 sts + 1 on a background of rev st st.

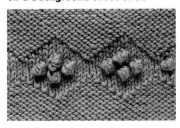

ROW 1 (RS): P5, ▶ K1, P9, rep from ▶ to last 6 sts, K1, P5.

ROW 2: K4, ▶ P3, K7, rep from ▶ to last 7 sts, P3, K4.

ROW 3: P3, ▶ K5, P5, rep from ▶ to last 8 sts, K5, P3.

ROW 4: K2, ▶ P7, K3, rep from ▶ to last 9 sts, P7, K2.

ROW 5: P1, ▶ K9, P1, rep from ▶ to end.

ROWS 6, 8 & 10: Purl.

ROWS 7 & 11: K5, make bobble (MB) as foll: (K1, yo, K1 into next st, turn, P3, turn, K3, turn, purl, sl1, K2tog, psso) K9, rep from ▶ to 6 sts, MB, K5.

ROW 9: K3, ▶ MB, K3, MB, K5, rep from ▶ to last 8 sts, MB, K3, MB, K3.

ROW 12: K1, ▶ P9, K1, rep from ▶ to end.

ROW 13: P2, ▶ K7, P3, rep from ▶ to last 9 sts, K7, P2.

ROW 14: K3, ▶ P5, K5, rep from ▶ to last 8 sts, P5, K3.

ROW 15: P4, ▶ K3, P7, rep from ▶ to last 7 sts, K3, P4.

ROW 16: K5, ▶ P1, K9, rep from ▶ to last 6 sts, P1, K5.

LARGE BOBBLE WITH EYELETS
Work with a multiple of 9 sts + 1 on a background of st st.

ROW 1 (RS): Knit.

ROW 2 & EVERY ALT ROW: Purl.

ROW 3 & 9: K4, ▶ yo, K2tog, K7, rep from ▶ to last 6 sts, yo, K2tog, K4.

ROW 5: Knit.

ROW 7: K2, ▶ yo, K2tog, K1, make bobble (MB) as foll: (K1, P1, K1,

P1, K1 into next st, turn, K5, turn, P5, turn, K5, turn, lift second, third, fourth and fifth sts over the first, turn), K1, yo, K2tog, K3, rep from ▶ to last 7sts, yo, K2tog, MB, K1, yo, K2tog, K1.

ROW 11: Knit.

ROW 12: Purl.

SINGLE FLOWER
Work with a multiple of 13 sts on a background of rev st st.

ROWS 1, 3, 5 & 7 (RS): P6, K1b, P6.

ROWS 2, 4, 6, 8 & 10: K6, P1b, K6.

ROWS 9: P2, insert point of right-hand needle from front through fabric to right of twisted K st in first row, catch yarn and draw through a long, loose loop, slip this loop onto right-hand needle, K next st and pass the loop over st, P3, K1b, P2, draw through another loop from left of same st in first row, sl the loop onto right-hand needle, K next st and pass loop over, P3.

ROW 11: P6, (K1, yo) 3 times and K1 all in the same st, making 7 sts from one, P6.

ROW 12: K6, P7, K6.

ROW 13: P6, K2togb, K3, K2tog, P6.

Cast-on borders

These borders are worked from the cast-on stitches at the start of a piece of knitting. With the exception of the tubular rib, they can all also be worked before casting off on a collar or neckband. (*See 'Working with repeat patterns', page 82.*). Edging depths are based on working with a medium-weight cotton.

NO BORDER

For this variation, use the smaller needles to cast on the same number of stitches as stated in the pattern. Beginning with a knit row, work in stocking (stockinette) stitch for 2 rows, then change to the larger needles.

K1, P1 RIB BORDER
Work with a multiple of 2 sts + 1.

ROW 1 (RS): K1, ▶ P1, K1, rep from ▶ to end.

ROW 2: P1, ▶ K1, P1, rep from ▶ to end.

K2, P2 RIB BORDER
Work with a multiple of 4 sts + 2.

ROW 1 (RS): K2, ▶ P2, K2, rep from ▶ to end.

ROW 2: P2, ▶ K2, P2, rep from ▶ to end.

These 2 rows form the repeat.

TUBULAR K1, P1 RIB BORDER
Cast on half the number of stitches needed plus 1.

ROW 1 (WS): With waste yarn, purl.

ROW 2: Knit.

ROWS 3 & 5: Change to main colour, purl.

ROWS 4 & 6: Knit.

Row 7: ▶ P1, pick up loop from first row of main colour using right needle. Transfer loop from right to left needle and K it.

Rep from ▶ to end.

Cont in rib as set. You may need to inc one extra st if an even number of sts is required. Undo the contrasting yarn by drawing the loose end up tight and cutting it. The first few stitches will separate from the main section of knitting. Repeat this process until only the main yarn remains.

RIDGED RIB

Work with a multiple of 3 sts.

ROWS 1 & 3 (RS): ▶ K2, P1, rep from ▶ to end of row.
ROW 2: ▶ K1, P2, rep from ▶ to end of row.
ROW 4: Knit.

SMALL TWISTED RIB BORDER

Work with a multiple of 4 sts + 2.

ROW 1 (RS): P2, ▶ K2, P2, rep from ▶ to end.
ROWS 2 & 4: K2, ▶ P2, K2 rep from ▶ to end
ROW 3: P2, ▶ C2B, P2, rep from ▶ to end.
These 4 rows form the repeat.

STOCKING (STOCKINETTE) STITCH AND K2 P2 RIB

Work with a multiple of 4 sts + 2.

ROWS 1 & 3 (RS): Knit.
ROWS 2 & 4: Purl.
ROW 5: ▶ K2, P2, rep from ▶ to last 2 sts K2.
ROW 6: ▶ P2, K2, rep from ▶ to last 2 sts P2.
Rep rows 5 & 6 to the required length.

GARTER STITCH BORDER

To work this border, simply knit every row.

MOSS (SEED) STITCH BORDER

Work with a multiple of 2 sts.

ROW 1 (RS): K1, P1 rep from ▶ to end.
ROW 2: P1, K1 rep from ▶ to end
These 2 rows form the repeat.

Simple cast-on and cast-off edgings

FRILL CAST-ON

Cast on 4 times the number of sts needed for main garment minus 3.

ROW 1 (RS): K1, ▶ K2, slip first st over second st on right needle, rep from ▶ to end.
ROW 2: P1, ▶ P2tog, rep from ▶ to end.

DECORATIVE CAST-OFF

To cast off a multiple of 3 sts + 2.

Cast off 2 sts, ▶ slip remaining st on right-hand needle back onto left-hand needle, cast on 2 sts, cast off 4 sts; rep from ▶ to end, fasten off rem st.

PICOT CAST-ON AND CAST-OFF

Work with a multiple of 2 sts.

ROWS 1, 3, 7 & 9 (RS): Knit.
ROWS 2, 4, 6 & 8: Purl.

ROW 5: ▶ K2tog, yo, rep from ▶ to last two sts, K2tog.
Fold the edging in half and slipstitch it ino place.

Decorative edgings

CABLED RIB

Work with a multiple of 10 sts + 2.

ROW 1: ▶ K2, P2, K4, P2, rep from ▶ to last 2 sts, K2.
ROW 2: P2, ▶ K2, P4, K2, P2, rep from ▶ to end.
ROW 3: ▶ K2, P2, C4B, P2, rep from ▶ to last 2 sts, K2.
ROW 4: P2, ▶ K2, P4, K2, P2 rep from ▶ to end.
Rep these two rows until work measures the required length.

ZIGZAG EDGING

Cast on 2 sts using the thumb method

ROW 1 (RS): K2.
ROW 2: Yo, K2.
ROW 3: Yo, K3.
ROW 4: Yo, K4.
ROW 5: Yo, K5.
ROW 6: Yo, K6.
ROW 7: Yo, K7.

ROW 8: Yo, K8.

Row 9: Yo, K9 *(10 sts)*. Break yarn and leave point on needle. On the same needle cast on 2 sts and work 2nd point as first. Work number of points needed. On last point do not break yarn but turn and knit across all points on needle. More or fewer rows can be worked, depending on size of point required.

PLEATED EDGING

Work with a multiple of 12 sts + 3. Edging depth 5cm (2in).

Note: 2 sts are decreased for every repeat on 3rd and following alt rows. Once the

edging is finished the total number of stitches should be a multiple of 4 sts + 3.

ROW 1 (RS): P3, ▶ K9, P3, rep from ▶ to end.

ROW 2: K3, ▶ P9, K3, rep from ▶ to end.

ROW 3: P3, ▶ yb, sl1 K1 psso, K5, K2tog, P3, rep from ▶ to end.

ROW 4: K3, ▶ P7, K3, rep from ▶ to end.

ROW 5: P3, ▶ yb, sl1 K1 psso, K3, K2tog, P3, rep from ▶ to end.

ROW 6: K3, ▶ P5, K3, rep from ▶ to end.

ROW 7: P3, ▶ yb, sl1 K1 psso, K1, K2tog, P3, rep from ▶ to end.

Row 8: K3, ▶ P3, K3, rep from ▶ to end.

ROW 9: P3, ▶ yb, sl1, K2tog, psso, P3, rep from ▶ to end.

ROW 10: K3, ▶ P1, K3, rep from ▶ to end.

ROW 11: P3, ▶ K1, P3, rep from ▶ to end.

ROW 12: K3, ▶ P1, K3, rep from ▶ to end.

These 12 rows form the edging.

EYELET EDGING

Cast on multiple of 2 sts + 1. Edging depth 2.5cm (1in).

Worked on a background of st st.

ROW 1 (RS): Knit.

ROWS 2 & 3: Knit.

ROW 4: ▶ P2tog, yo; rep from ▶ to last st, P1.

ROWS 5, 6 & 7: Knit.

ROW 8: Purl.

Lengthways lace edging

These lace edging are worked separately. Join all the seams first. Work the edging until it is long enough to fit all the way around the lower edge of the garment when slightly stretched, then slipstitched into position. Edging depths are based on working with a medium-weight cotton.

SHALLOW EYELET EDGING

Worked lengthways over 6 sts. Edging depth 3cm (1¼in).

Note: Stitches should be counted only after the 4th row.

ROW 1 (RS): K1, K2tog, yo, K2, (yo) twice, K1.

ROW 2: K2, K1 tbl, K2tog, yo, K3.

ROW 3: K1, K2tog, yo, K5.

ROW 4: Cast off 2 sts leaving 1 st on right-hand needle, K2tog, yo, K3. These 4 rows form the repeat.

LEAFY EDGING

Worked lengthwise over 8 sts. Edging depth 6cm (2½in).

Note: Stitches should be counted only after the 18th row.

ROW 1 (RS): K5, yo, K1, yo, K2.

ROW 2: P6, inc in next st by knitting into front and back of it, K3.

ROW 3: K4, P1, K2, yo, K1, yo, K3.

ROW 4: P8, inc in next st, K4.

ROW 5: K4, P2, K3, yo, K1, yo, K4.

ROW 6: P10, inc in next st, K5.

ROW 7: K4, P3, K4, yo, K1, yo, K5.

ROW 8: P12, inc in next st, K6.

ROW 9: K4, P4, yb, sl1 K1 psso, K7, K2tog, K1.

ROW 10: P10, inc in next st, K7.

ROW 11: K4, P5, yb, sl1 K1 psso, K5, K2tog, K1.

ROW 12: P8, inc in next st, K2, P1, K5.

ROW 13: K4, P1, K1, P4, yb, sl1 K1 psso, K3, K2tog, K1.

ROW 14: P6, inc in next st, K3, P1, K5.

ROW 15: K4, P1, K1, P5, yb, sl1 K1 psso, K1, K2tog, K1.

ROW 16: P4, inc in next st, K4, P1, K5.

ROW 17: K4, P1, K1, P6, yb, sl1, K2tog, psso, K1.

ROW 18: P2tog, cast off 5 sts using P2tog as first of these sts (1 st on right-hand needle), K1, P1, K5.

These 18 rows form the repeat.

POINTED EDGING

Worked lengthwise over 8 sts Edging depth 7cm (2¾).

Note: Stitches should be counted only after the 12th row.

FOUNDATION ROW: Knit.

ROW 1 (RS): Sl1, K1, (yo, K2tog)

twice, yo, K2.

ROW 2: K2, yo, K2, (yo, K2tog) twice, K1.

ROW 3: Sl1, K1, (yo, K2tog) twice, K2, yo, K2.

ROW 4: K2, yo, K4, (yo, K2tog) twice, K1.

ROW 5: Sl1, K1, (yo, K2tog) twice, K4, yo, K2.

ROW 6: K2, yo, K6, (yo, K2tog) twice, K1.

ROW 7: Sl1, K1, (yo, K2tog) twice, K6, yo, K2.

ROW 8: K2, yo, K8, (yo, K2tog) twice, K1.

ROW 9: Sl1, K1, (yo, K2tog) twice, K8, yo, K2.

ROW 10: K2, yo, K10, (yo, K2tog) twice, K1.

ROW 11: Sl1, K1, (yo, K2tog) twice, K10, yo, K2.

ROW 12: Cast off 11 sts, leaving 1 st on right-hand needle, K2, (yo, K2tog) twice, K1.

These 12 rows form the repeat.

POINTED ZIGZAG EYELET EDGING

Worked lengthwise over 12 sts.

Edging depth 8cm (3in).

Note: *Stitches should be counted only after the 16th row.*

ROW 1 (WS): Sl1, K3, yo, K2tog, K2, yo, K2tog, yo, K2.

ROW 2: Yo, K2tog, K11.

ROW 3: Sl1, K2, (yo, K2tog) twice, K2, yo, K2tog, yo, K2.

ROW 4: Yo, K2tog, K12.

ROW 5: Sl1, K3, (yo, K2tog) twice, K2, yo, K2tog, yo, K2.

ROW 6: Yo, K2tog, K13.

ROW 7: Sl1, K2, (yo, K2tog) 3 times, K2, yo, K2tog, yo, K2.

ROW 8: Yo, K2tog, K14.

ROW 9: Sl1, K2, (K2tog, yo) twice, K2, K2tog, (yo, K2tog) twice, K1.

ROW 10: Yo, K2tog, K13.

ROW 11: Sl1, K1, (K2tog, yo) twice, K2, K2tog, (yo, K2tog) twice, K1.

ROW 12: Yo, K2tog, K12.

ROW 13: Sl1, K2, K2tog, yo, K2, K2tog, (yo, K2tog) twice, K1.

ROW 14: Yo, K2tog, K11.

ROW 15: Sl1, K1, K2tog, yo, K2, K2tog, (yo, K2tog) twice K1.

ROW 16: Yo, K2tog, K10.

These 16 rows form the repeat.

DIAMOND EDGING

Worked lengthwise over 9 sts.

Edging depth 6cm (2½in).

Note: *Stitches should be counted only after the first or 12th rows.*

ROW 1 AND EVERY ALT ROW (RS): Knit.

ROW 2: K3, (K2tog, yo) twice, K1, yo, K1.

ROW 4: K2, (K2tog, yo) twice, K3, yo, K1.

ROW 6: K1, (K2tog, yo) twice, K5, yo, K1.

ROW 8: K3, (yo, K2tog) twice, K1, K2tog, yo, K2tog.

ROW 10: K4, yo, K2tog, yo, K3tog, yo, K2tog.

ROW 12: K5, yo, K3tog, yo, K2tog.

These 12 rows form the repeat.

CIRCLE EYELETS WITH ZIGZAG EDGING

Worked lengthwise over 12 sts.

Edging depth 6cm (2½in).

Note: *Stitches should be counted only after the 14th row.*

ROW 1 (RS): K1, yo, K2tog , K6, K2tog, yo, K1.

ROW 2: K12.

ROW 3: K1, yo, K2, K2tog, (yo) twice, K2tog, K2, yo, K2tog, K1.

ROW 4: K7, yo, K2tog, K4.

ROW 5: K1, yo, K1, K2tog, (yo) twice, (K2tog) twice, (yo) twice, K2tog, yo, K2tog, K1.

ROW 6: K5, yo, K2tog, K2, yo, K2tog, K3.

ROW 7: K1, yo, K4, K2tog, (yo) twice, K2 tog, K2, yo, K2tog, K1.

ROW 8: K7, yo, K2tog, K6.

ROW 9: K1, yo, K3tog, K2tog, (yo) twice (K2tog) twice, (yo) twice, K2tog, yo, K2tog, K1.

ROW 10: K5, yo, K2tog, K2, yo, K2tog, K3.

ROW 11: K1, yo, K3tog, K1, K2tog, (yo) twice, K2tog, K2, yo, K2tog, K1.

ROW 12: K7, yo, K2tog, K4.

ROW 13: K1, yo, K3tog, K6, yo, K2tog, K1.

ROW 14: K12.

These 14 rows form the repeat.

SMALL POINTED EDGING WITH EYELET STRIPES

Worked lengthwise over 11 sts.

Edging depth 6cm (2½in).

Note: *Stitches should be counted only after the 4th row.*

FOUNDATION ROW: Knit.

ROW 1 (RS): K3, (yo, sl1 K1 psso, K1) twice, (yo) twice, K1, (yo) twice, K1.

ROW 2: (K2, P1) 4 times, K3. (On this row each double yo is treated as 2 sts, the first being knitted, the second purled.)

ROW 3: K3, yo, sl1 K1 psso, K1, yo, sl1 K1 psso, K7.

ROW 4: Cast off 4 sts, leaving 1 st on right-hand needle, K3, P1, K2, P1, K3.

These 4 rows form the repeat.

Motif library

Choose from a roaring lion, a dancing skeleton or a farmyard dog. Pick one motif and combine it with masses of others from the huge range of themed motifs in this library – the choice is totally up to you. The motifs are here to spark your imagination and to let it run riot. Whatever motifs you choose to knit, your child can feel that they have a garment that is unique to them and will be the envy of their friends.

Geometric repeat patterns

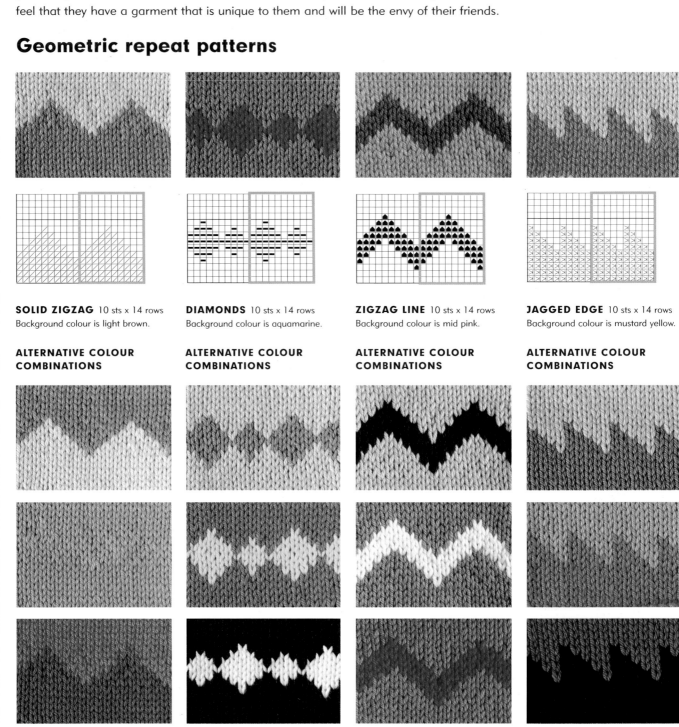

⊡	LIGHT KHAKI
▶	MID GREEN
□	AQUAMARINE
△	LIGHT BLUE
⊠	PASTEL BLUE
↑	PALE GREY
⬟	BLUE
■	NAVY BLUE
╱	PURPLE
✳	DEEP PINK
∧	MID PINK
╱	PASTEL PINK
▬	RED
▷	DEEP ORANGE
┼	BRIGHT YELLOW
○	MUSTARD
⊥	BRIGHT GREEN
╱	OLD GOLD
★	LIGHT BROWN
◇	BEIGE
◺	PALE YELLOW
●	ECRU
╱	WHITE
▼	GREY
●	BLACK

SOLID ZIGZAG 10 sts x 14 rows
Background colour is light brown.

DIAMONDS 10 sts x 14 rows
Background colour is aquamarine.

ZIGZAG LINE 10 sts x 14 rows
Background colour is mid pink.

JAGGED EDGE 10 sts x 14 rows
Background colour is mustard yellow.

ALTERNATIVE COLOUR COMBINATIONS

ALTERNATIVE COLOUR COMBINATIONS

ALTERNATIVE COLOUR COMBINATIONS

ALTERNATIVE COLOUR COMBINATIONS

CROSS STRIP 10 sts x 14 rows Background colour is purple.

NOUGHTS & CROSSES 10 sts x 14 rows Background colour is bright green.

DOUGHNUT STRIP 10 sts x 14 rows Background colour is red.

ZIGZAG STRIP 10 sts x 14 rows Background colour is light blue.

DIAMOND STRIP 10 sts x 14 rows Background colour is bright green.

HEART STRIP 20 sts x 14 rows Background colour is ecru.

LIGHT KHAKI

MID GREEN

AQUAMARINE

LIGHT BLUE

PASTEL BLUE

PALE GREY

BLUE

NAVY BLUE

PURPLE

DEEP PINK

MID PINK

PASTEL PINK

RED

DEEP ORANGE

BRIGHT YELLOW

MUSTARD

BRIGHT GREEN

OLD GOLD

LIGHT BROWN

BEIGE

PALE YELLOW

ECRU

WHITE

GREY

BLACK

Geometric designs and shapes

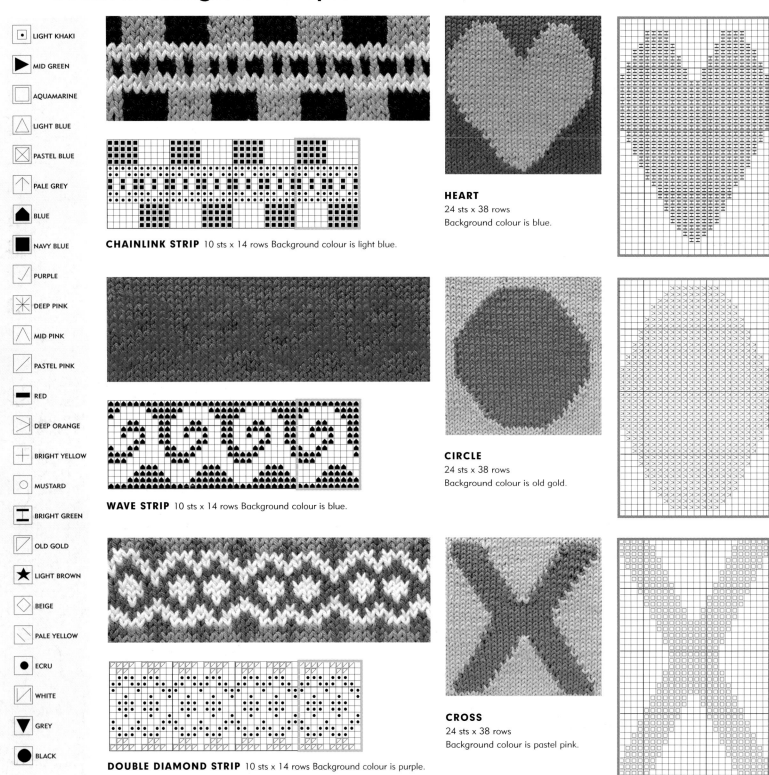

Legend (key):

- ⊡ LIGHT KHAKI
- ▶ MID GREEN
- ▢ AQUAMARINE
- △ LIGHT BLUE
- ⊠ PASTEL BLUE
- ↑ PALE GREY
- ⬟ BLUE
- ■ NAVY BLUE
- ╱ PURPLE
- ✳ DEEP PINK
- ⋀ MID PINK
- ╱ PASTEL PINK
- ▬ RED
- ⧄ DEEP ORANGE
- ✛ BRIGHT YELLOW
- ○ MUSTARD
- ⌶ BRIGHT GREEN
- ╱ OLD GOLD
- ★ LIGHT BROWN
- ◇ BEIGE
- ╲ PALE YELLOW
- ● ECRU
- ╱ WHITE
- ▼ GREY
- ● BLACK

CHAINLINK STRIP 10 sts x 14 rows Background colour is light blue.

WAVE STRIP 10 sts x 14 rows Background colour is blue.

DOUBLE DIAMOND STRIP 10 sts x 14 rows Background colour is purple.

HEART
24 sts x 38 rows
Background colour is blue.

CIRCLE
24 sts x 38 rows
Background colour is old gold.

CROSS
24 sts x 38 rows
Background colour is pastel pink.

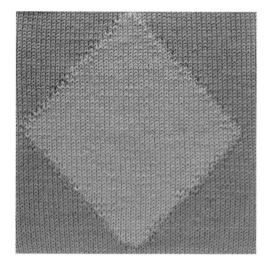

DIAMOND
50 sts x 70 rows
Background
colour is
aquamarine.

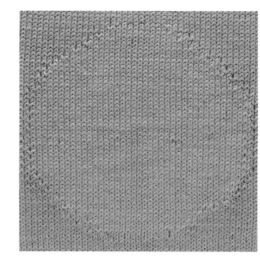

SOCCER BALL
50 sts x 70 rows
Background
colour is purple.

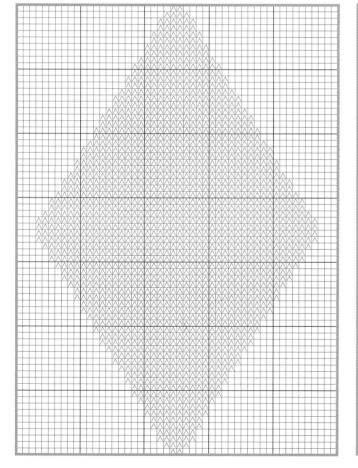

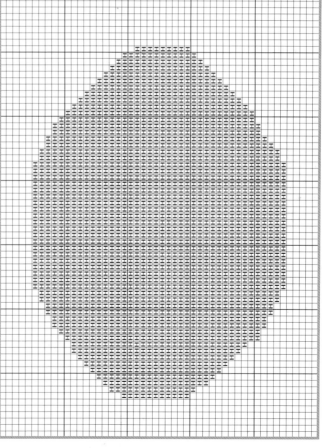

LIGHT KHAKI

MID GREEN

AQUAMARINE

LIGHT BLUE

PASTEL BLUE

PALE GREY

BLUE

NAVY BLUE

PURPLE

DEEP PINK

MID PINK

PASTEL PINK

RED

DEEP ORANGE

BRIGHT YELLOW

MUSTARD

BRIGHT GREEN

OLD GOLD

LIGHT BROWN

BEIGE

PALE YELLOW

ECRU

WHITE

GREY

BLACK

Letters and numbers

ALPHABET, PUNCTUATION AND NUMBERS 10 sts x 14 rows. Background colour is aquamarine.

⊡	LIGHT KHAKI
▶	MID GREEN
☐	AQUAMARINE
△	LIGHT BLUE
⊠	PASTEL BLUE
↑	PALE GREY
⬟	BLUE
■	NAVY BLUE
◹	PURPLE
✳	DEEP PINK
⋀	MID PINK
◿	PASTEL PINK
▬	RED
◩	DEEP ORANGE
⊞	BRIGHT YELLOW
◯	MUSTARD
⌶	BRIGHT GREEN
◸	OLD GOLD
★	LIGHT BROWN
◇	BEIGE
◺	PALE YELLOW
●	ECRU
◹	WHITE
▼	GREY
⬤	BLACK

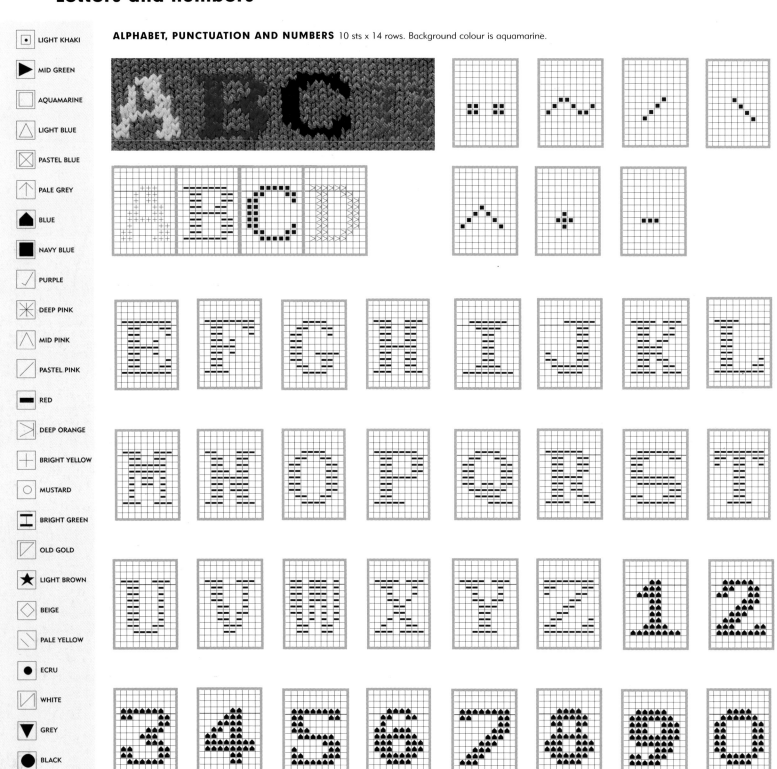

Food

ICE LOLLY
10 sts x 14 rows
Background
colour is
pastel blue.

SLICED KIWI
10 sts x 14 rows
Background
colour is ecru.

RED APPLE
10 sts x 14 rows
Background
colour is purple.

CARROT
10 sts x 14 rows
Background
colour is
pale yellow.

BUNCH OF BANANAS
24 sts x 38 rows
Background colour is grey.

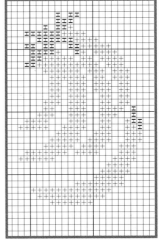

WATERMELON
24 sts x 38 rows
Background colour is pastel pink.

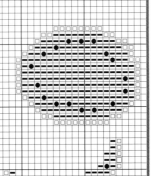

BIRTHDAY CAKE
24 sts x 38 rows
Background colour is light blue.

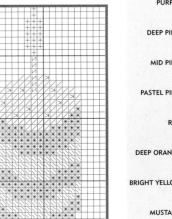

FRIED EGG
24 sts x 38 rows
Background colour is deep orange.

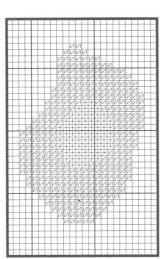

ICE CREAM CONE
24 sts x 38 rows
Background colour is mid pink.

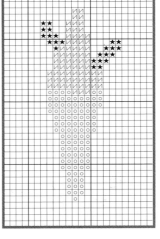

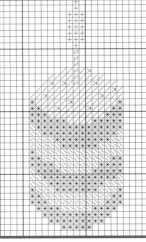

LIGHT KHAKI

MID GREEN

AQUAMARINE

LIGHT BLUE

PASTEL BLUE

PALE GREY

BLUE

NAVY BLUE

PURPLE

DEEP PINK

MID PINK

PASTEL PINK

RED

DEEP ORANGE

BRIGHT YELLOW

MUSTARD

BRIGHT GREEN

OLD GOLD

LIGHT BROWN

BEIGE

PALE YELLOW

ECRU

WHITE

GREY

BLACK

High in the sky

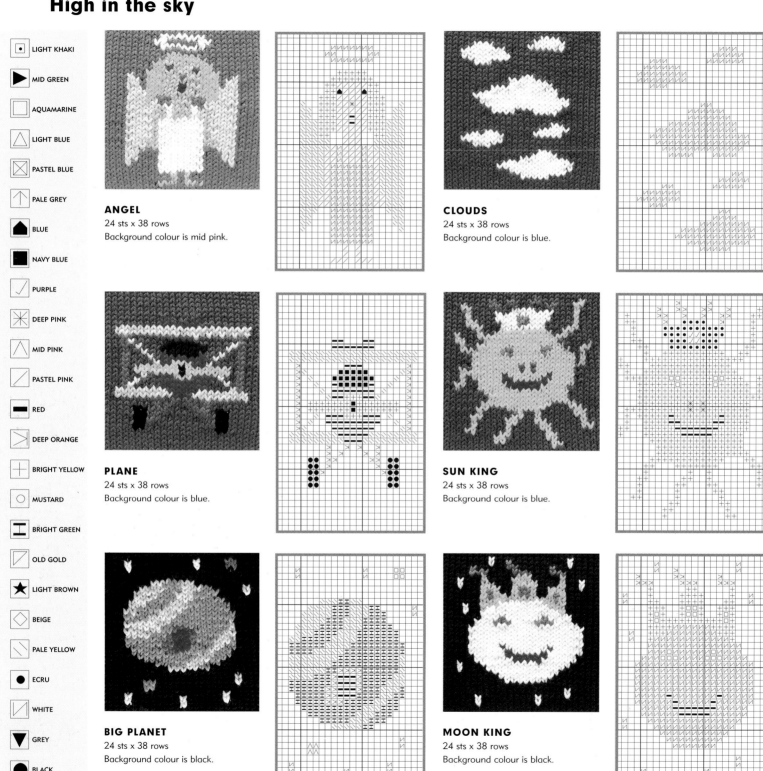

LIGHT KHAKI

MID GREEN

AQUAMARINE

LIGHT BLUE

PASTEL BLUE

PALE GREY

BLUE

NAVY BLUE

PURPLE

DEEP PINK

MID PINK

PASTEL PINK

RED

DEEP ORANGE

BRIGHT YELLOW

MUSTARD

BRIGHT GREEN

OLD GOLD

LIGHT BROWN

BEIGE

PALE YELLOW

ECRU

WHITE

GREY

BLACK

ANGEL
24 sts x 38 rows
Background colour is mid pink.

CLOUDS
24 sts x 38 rows
Background colour is blue.

PLANE
24 sts x 38 rows
Background colour is blue.

SUN KING
24 sts x 38 rows
Background colour is blue.

BIG PLANET
24 sts x 38 rows
Background colour is black.

MOON KING
24 sts x 38 rows
Background colour is black.

SLEEPING MOON
24 sts x 38 rows
Background colour is black.

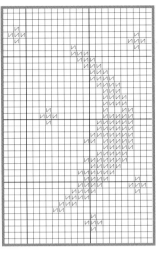

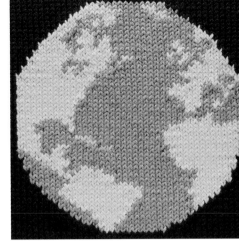

EARTH
50 sts x 70 rows
Background
colour is black.

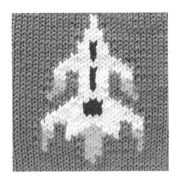

ROCKET SHIP
24 sts x 38 rows
Background colour is light blue.

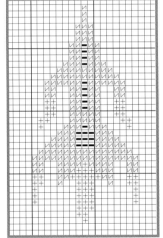

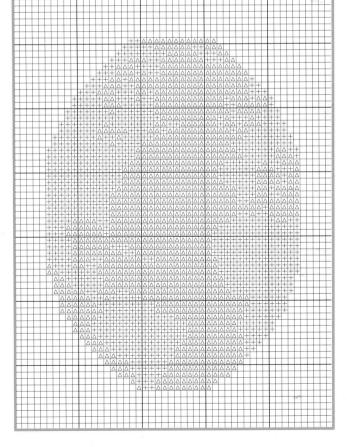

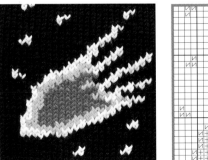

COMET
24 sts x 38 rows
Background colour is black.

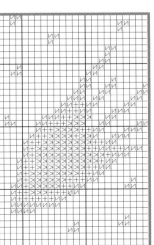

LIGHT KHAKI

MID GREEN

AQUAMARINE

LIGHT BLUE

PASTEL BLUE

PALE GREY

BLUE

NAVY BLUE

PURPLE

DEEP PINK

MID PINK

PASTEL PINK

RED

DEEP ORANGE

BRIGHT YELLOW

MUSTARD

BRIGHT GREEN

OLD GOLD

LIGHT BROWN

BEIGE

PALE YELLOW

ECRU

WHITE

GREY

BLACK

Scary stories

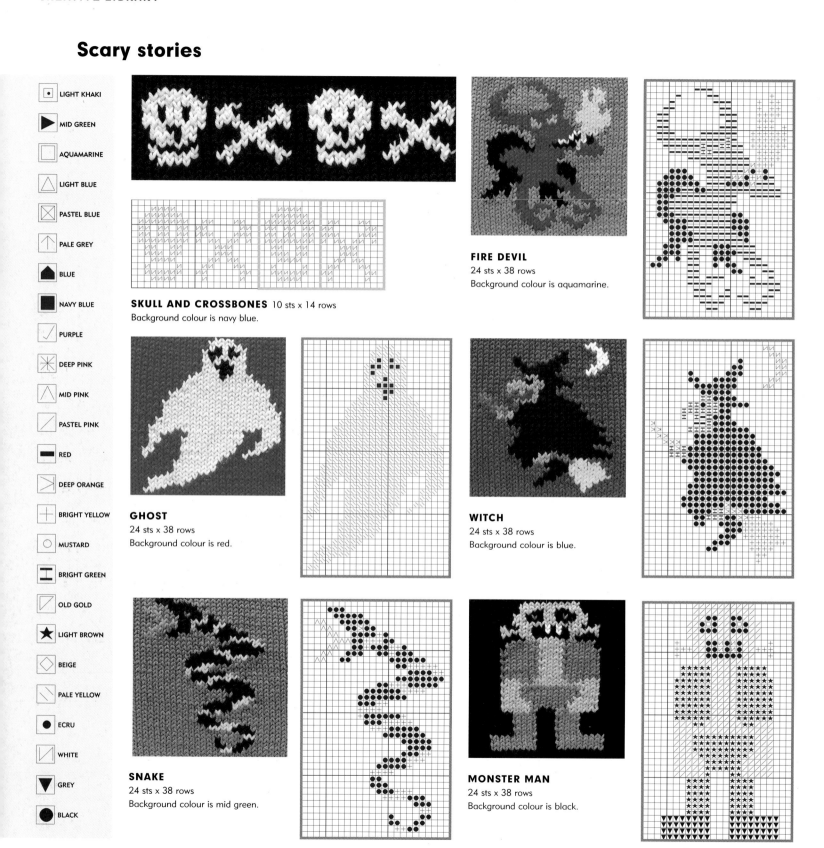

LIGHT KHAKI

MID GREEN

AQUAMARINE

LIGHT BLUE

PASTEL BLUE

PALE GREY

BLUE

NAVY BLUE

PURPLE

DEEP PINK

MID PINK

PASTEL PINK

RED

DEEP ORANGE

BRIGHT YELLOW

MUSTARD

BRIGHT GREEN

OLD GOLD

LIGHT BROWN

BEIGE

PALE YELLOW

ECRU

WHITE

GREY

BLACK

SKULL AND CROSSBONES 10 sts x 14 rows
Background colour is navy blue.

FIRE DEVIL
24 sts x 38 rows
Background colour is aquamarine.

GHOST
24 sts x 38 rows
Background colour is red.

WITCH
24 sts x 38 rows
Background colour is blue.

SNAKE
24 sts x 38 rows
Background colour is mid green.

MONSTER MAN
24 sts x 38 rows
Background colour is black.

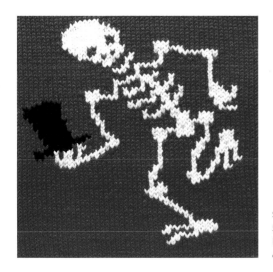

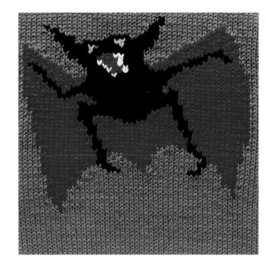

SKELETON
50 sts x 70 rows
Background
colour is red.

BAT
50 sts x 70 rows
Background
colour is
mid green.

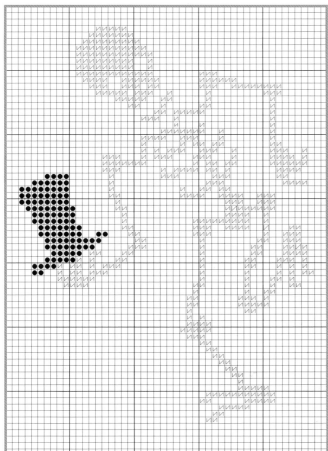

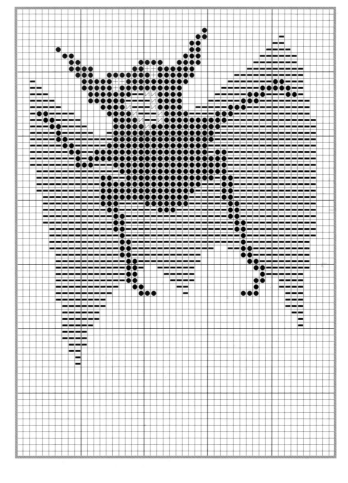

LIGHT KHAKI

MID GREEN

AQUAMARINE

LIGHT BLUE

PASTEL BLUE

PALE GREY

BLUE

NAVY BLUE

PURPLE

DEEP PINK

MID PINK

PASTEL PINK

RED

DEEP ORANGE

BRIGHT YELLOW

MUSTARD

BRIGHT GREEN

OLD GOLD

LIGHT BROWN

BEIGE

PALE YELLOW

ECRU

WHITE

GREY

BLACK

Playtime

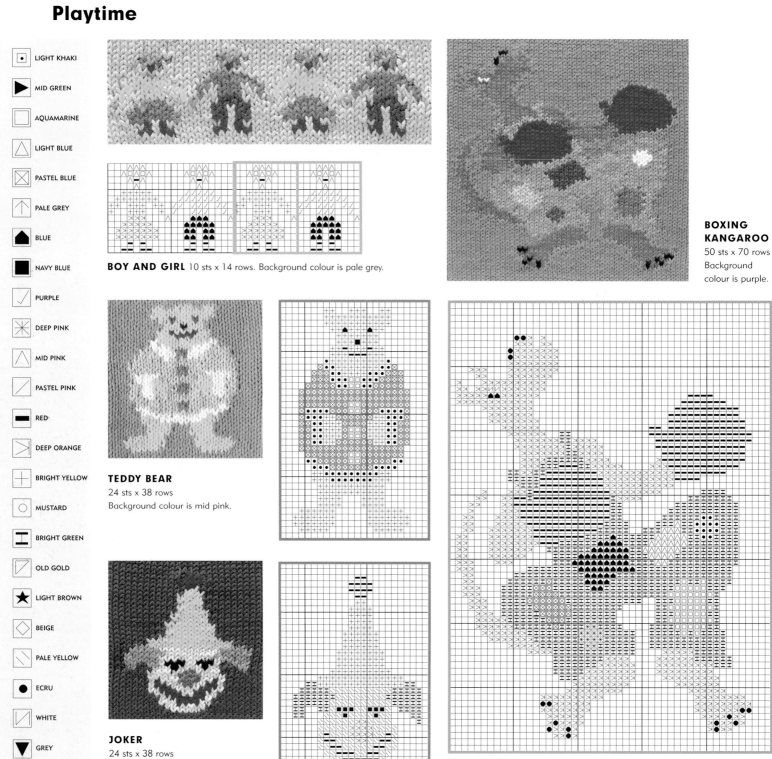

LIGHT KHAKI

MID GREEN

AQUAMARINE

LIGHT BLUE

PASTEL BLUE

PALE GREY

BLUE

NAVY BLUE

PURPLE

DEEP PINK

MID PINK

PASTEL PINK

RED

DEEP ORANGE

BRIGHT YELLOW

MUSTARD

BRIGHT GREEN

OLD GOLD

LIGHT BROWN

BEIGE

PALE YELLOW

ECRU

WHITE

GREY

BLACK

BOY AND GIRL 10 sts x 14 rows. Background colour is pale grey.

BOXING KANGAROO
50 sts x 70 rows
Background colour is purple.

TEDDY BEAR
24 sts x 38 rows
Background colour is mid pink.

JOKER
24 sts x 38 rows
Background colour is blue.

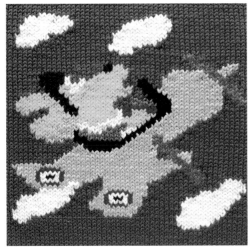

FIGHTER-PILOT DOG
50 sts x 70 rows
Background colour is blue.

COW JUMPING OVER THE MOON
50 sts x 70 rows
Background colour is light blue.

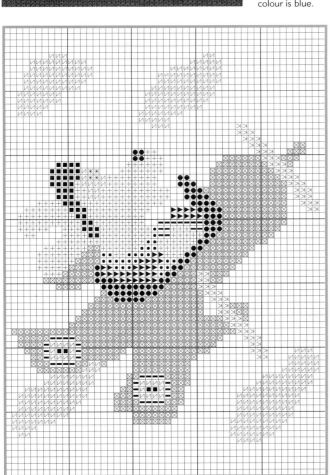

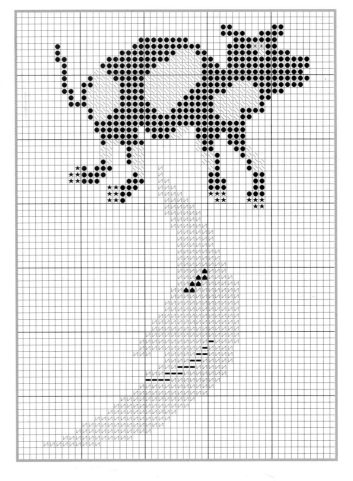

LIGHT KHAKI

MID GREEN

AQUAMARINE

LIGHT BLUE

PASTEL BLUE

PALE GREY

BLUE

NAVY BLUE

PURPLE

DEEP PINK

MID PINK

PASTEL PINK

RED

DEEP ORANGE

BRIGHT YELLOW

MUSTARD

BRIGHT GREEN

OLD GOLD

LIGHT BROWN

BEIGE

PALE YELLOW

ECRU

WHITE

GREY

BLACK

Playtime

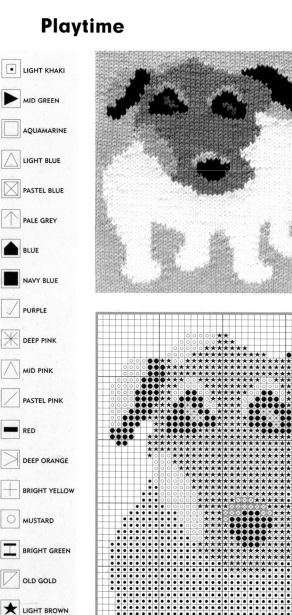

⊡	LIGHT KHAKI
▶	MID GREEN
□	AQUAMARINE
△	LIGHT BLUE
⊠	PASTEL BLUE
↑	PALE GREY
⬟	BLUE
◼	NAVY BLUE
✓	PURPLE
✳	DEEP PINK
∧	MID PINK
⟋	PASTEL PINK
▬	RED
⟍	DEEP ORANGE
✚	BRIGHT YELLOW
○	MUSTARD
⊥	BRIGHT GREEN
⟋	OLD GOLD
★	LIGHT BROWN
◇	BEIGE
⟍	PALE YELLOW
●	ECRU
◺	WHITE
▼	GREY
⬤	BLACK

BILLY DOG
50 sts x 70 rows
Background
colour is
pastel pink.

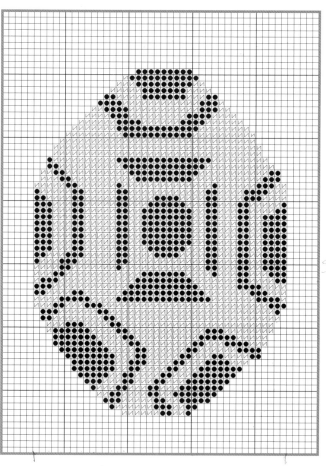

SOCCER BALL
50 sts x 70 rows
Background
colour is red.

Beside the seaside

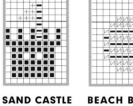

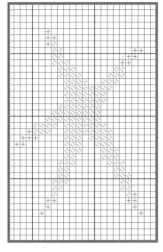

ANCHOR
10 sts x 14 rows
Background colour is mustard yellow.

FISH
10 sts x 14 rows
Background colour is light blue.

SAND CASTLE
10 sts x 14 rows
Background colour is pale yellow.

BEACH BALL
10 sts x 14 rows
Background colour is bright yellow.

STARFISH
24 sts x 38 rows
Background colour is aquamarine.

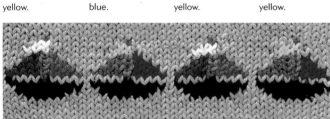

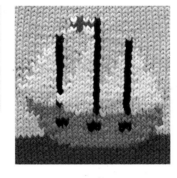

BOATS 10 sts x 14 rows Background colour is pale grey.

SAILING SHIP
24 sts x 38 rows
Background colour is pale grey.

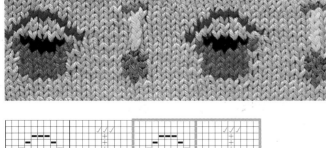

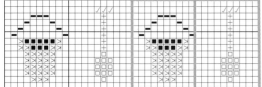

BUCKETS AND SPADES 10 sts x 14 rows Background colour is pale grey.

SURF DUDE
24 sts x 38 rows
Background colour is blue.

LIGHT KHAKI
MID GREEN
AQUAMARINE
LIGHT BLUE
PASTEL BLUE
PALE GREY
BLUE
NAVY BLUE
PURPLE
DEEP PINK
MID PINK
PASTEL PINK
RED
DEEP ORANGE
BRIGHT YELLOW
MUSTARD
BRIGHT GREEN
OLD GOLD
LIGHT BROWN
BEIGE
PALE YELLOW
ECRU
WHITE
GREY
BLACK

Swimming in the oceans

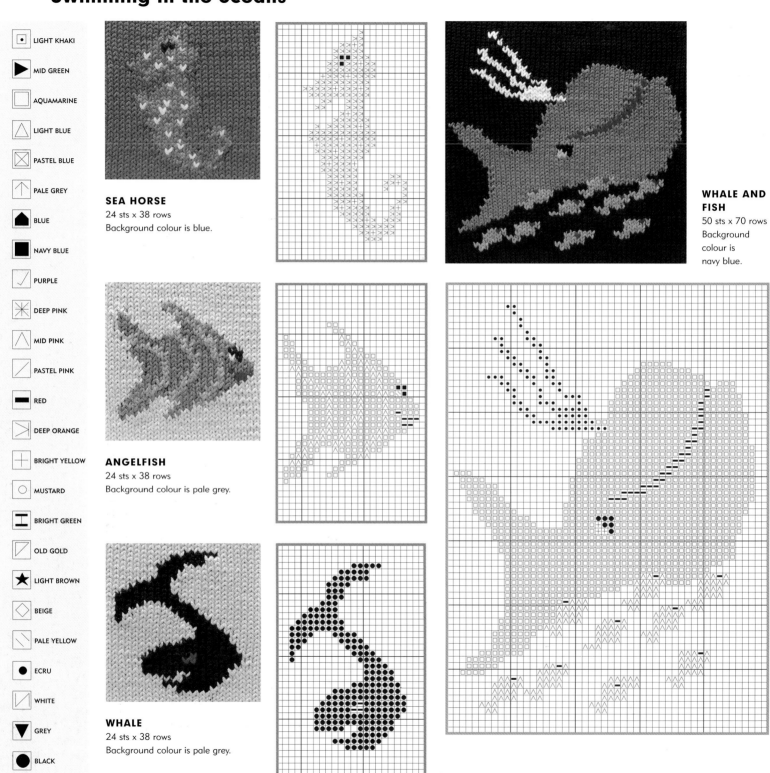

LIGHT KHAKI

MID GREEN

AQUAMARINE

LIGHT BLUE

PASTEL BLUE

PALE GREY

BLUE

NAVY BLUE

PURPLE

DEEP PINK

MID PINK

PASTEL PINK

RED

DEEP ORANGE

BRIGHT YELLOW

MUSTARD

BRIGHT GREEN

OLD GOLD

LIGHT BROWN

BEIGE

PALE YELLOW

ECRU

WHITE

GREY

BLACK

SEA HORSE
24 sts x 38 rows
Background colour is blue.

WHALE AND FISH
50 sts x 70 rows
Background colour is navy blue.

ANGELFISH
24 sts x 38 rows
Background colour is pale grey.

WHALE
24 sts x 38 rows
Background colour is pale grey.

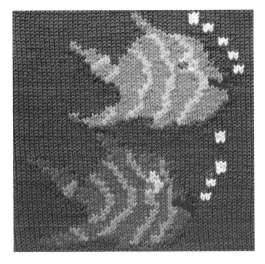

TROPICAL FISH
50 sts x 70 rows
Background colour is blue.

OCTOPUS
50 sts x 70 rows
Background colour is aquamarine.

LIGHT KHAKI

MID GREEN

AQUAMARINE

LIGHT BLUE

PASTEL BLUE

PALE GREY

BLUE

NAVY BLUE

PURPLE

DEEP PINK

MID PINK

PASTEL PINK

RED

DEEP ORANGE

BRIGHT YELLOW

MUSTARD

BRIGHT GREEN

OLD GOLD

LIGHT BROWN

BEIGE

PALE YELLOW

ECRU

WHITE

GREY

BLACK

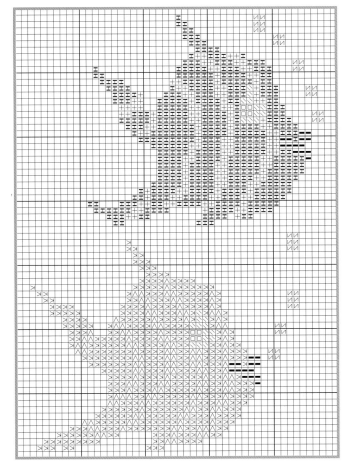

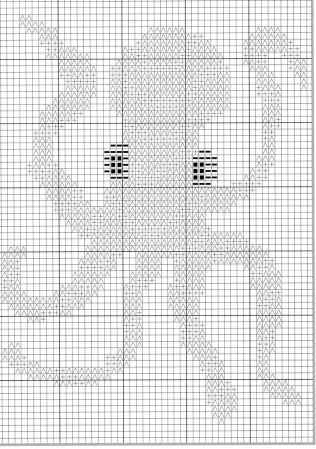

Circus and zoo

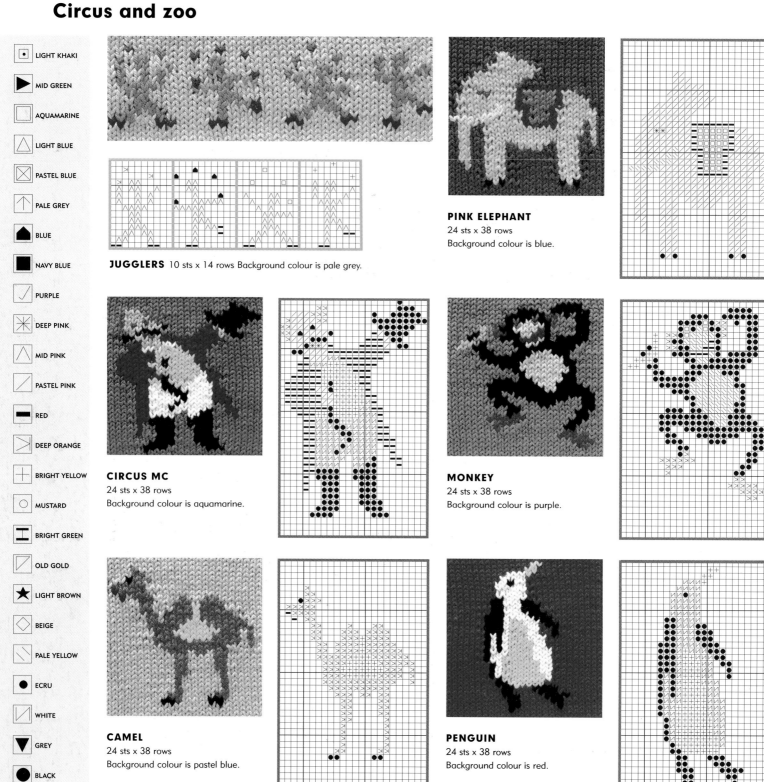

Key

⊡ LIGHT KHAKI

▶ MID GREEN

☐ AQUAMARINE

△ LIGHT BLUE

⊠ PASTEL BLUE

↑ PALE GREY

⬣ BLUE

■ NAVY BLUE

✓ PURPLE

✳ DEEP PINK

∧ MID PINK

╱ PASTEL PINK

▬ RED

⋈ DEEP ORANGE

+ BRIGHT YELLOW

○ MUSTARD

⊞ BRIGHT GREEN

╱ OLD GOLD

★ LIGHT BROWN

◇ BEIGE

⧄ PALE YELLOW

● ECRU

◺ WHITE

▼ GREY

● BLACK

JUGGLERS 10 sts x 14 rows Background colour is pale grey.

PINK ELEPHANT
24 sts x 38 rows
Background colour is blue.

CIRCUS MC
24 sts x 38 rows
Background colour is aquamarine.

MONKEY
24 sts x 38 rows
Background colour is purple.

CAMEL
24 sts x 38 rows
Background colour is pastel blue.

PENGUIN
24 sts x 38 rows
Background colour is red.

CLOWN
50 sts x 70 rows
Background
colour is
bright green.

**GIRL ON
A PONY**
50 sts x 70 rows
Background
colour is
pastel pink.

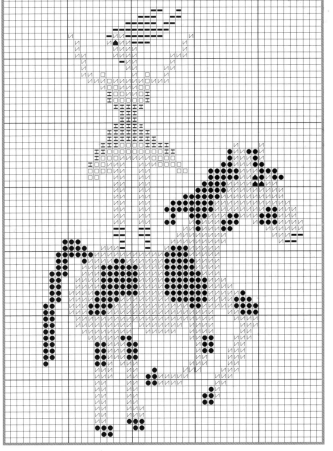

LIGHT KHAKI

MID GREEN

AQUAMARINE

LIGHT BLUE

PASTEL BLUE

PALE GREY

BLUE

NAVY BLUE

PURPLE

DEEP PINK

MID PINK

PASTEL PINK

RED

DEEP ORANGE

BRIGHT YELLOW

MUSTARD

BRIGHT GREEN

OLD GOLD

LIGHT BROWN

BEIGE

PALE YELLOW

ECRU

WHITE

GREY

BLACK

Circus and zoo

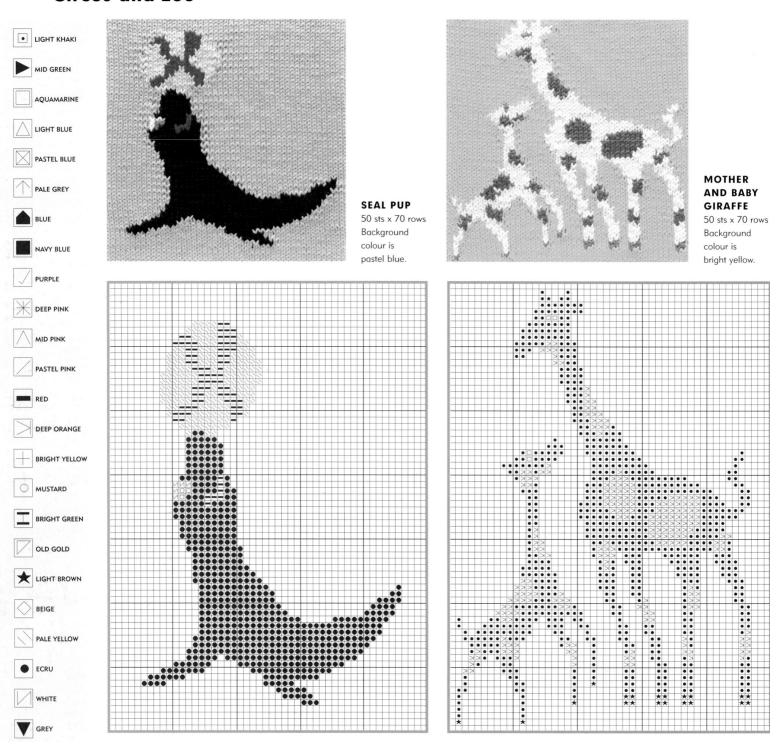

- ⊡ LIGHT KHAKI
- ▶ MID GREEN
- ☐ AQUAMARINE
- △ LIGHT BLUE
- ⊠ PASTEL BLUE
- ↑ PALE GREY
- ⬟ BLUE
- ■ NAVY BLUE
- ✓ PURPLE
- ✳ DEEP PINK
- ⋀ MID PINK
- ╱ PASTEL PINK
- ▬ RED
- ⋈ DEEP ORANGE
- ╫ BRIGHT YELLOW
- ○ MUSTARD
- ⊥ BRIGHT GREEN
- ╱ OLD GOLD
- ★ LIGHT BROWN
- ◇ BEIGE
- ╱ PALE YELLOW
- ● ECRU
- ╱ WHITE
- ▼ GREY
- ● BLACK

SEAL PUP
50 sts x 70 rows
Background
colour is
pastel blue.

**MOTHER
AND BABY
GIRAFFE**
50 sts x 70 rows
Background
colour is
bright yellow.

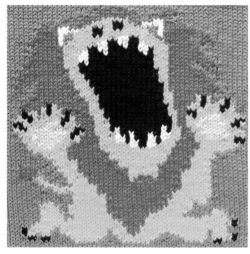

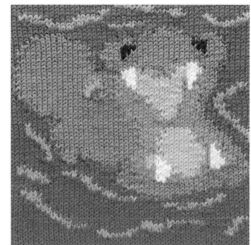

ROARING LION
50 sts x 70 rows
Background colour is grey.

HIPPO
50 sts x 70 rows
Background colour is blue.

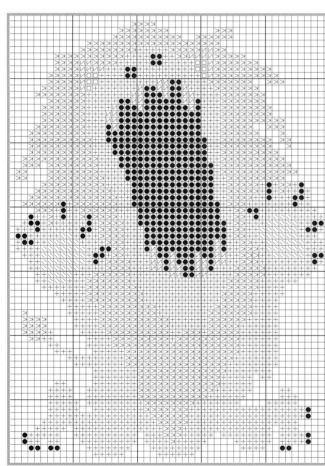

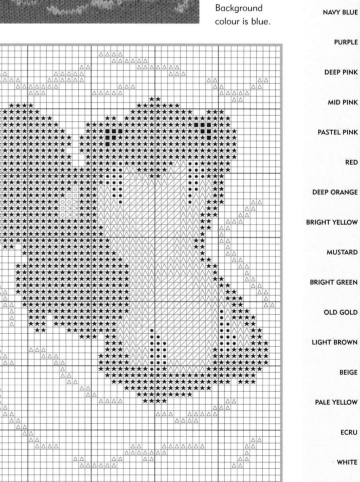

LIGHT KHAKI

MID GREEN

AQUAMARINE

LIGHT BLUE

PASTEL BLUE

PALE GREY

BLUE

NAVY BLUE

PURPLE

DEEP PINK

MID PINK

PASTEL PINK

RED

DEEP ORANGE

BRIGHT YELLOW

MUSTARD

BRIGHT GREEN

OLD GOLD

LIGHT BROWN

BEIGE

PALE YELLOW

ECRU

WHITE

GREY

BLACK

On the farm

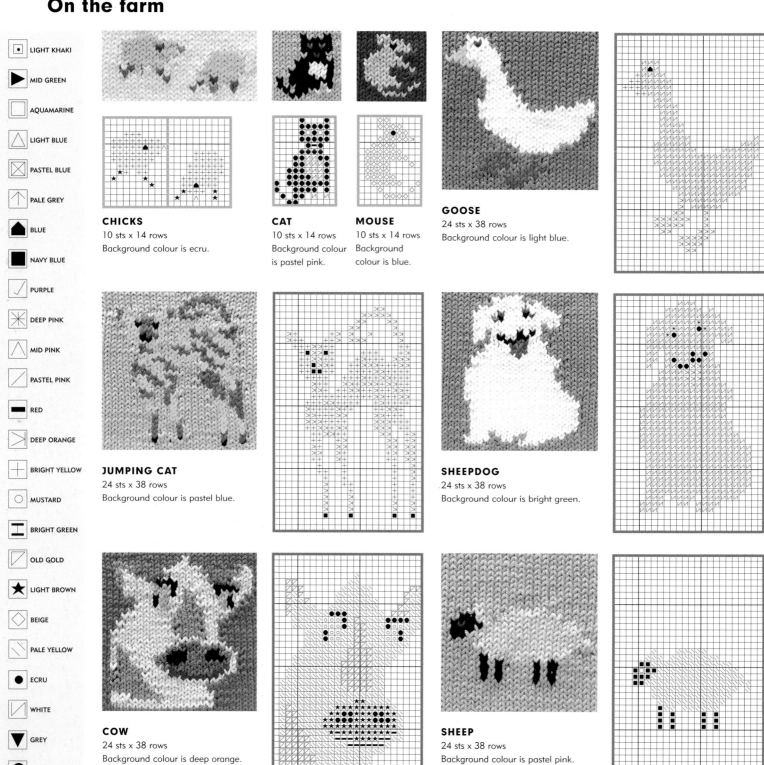

Key (left column):

- ⊡ LIGHT KHAKI
- ▶ MID GREEN
- ▢ AQUAMARINE
- △ LIGHT BLUE
- ⊠ PASTEL BLUE
- ↑ PALE GREY
- ⬟ BLUE
- ■ NAVY BLUE
- ╱ PURPLE
- ✳ DEEP PINK
- ∧ MID PINK
- ╱ PASTEL PINK
- ▬ RED
- ⧅ DEEP ORANGE
- ＋ BRIGHT YELLOW
- ○ MUSTARD
- ⊥ BRIGHT GREEN
- ╱ OLD GOLD
- ★ LIGHT BROWN
- ◇ BEIGE
- ╱ PALE YELLOW
- ● ECRU
- ◸ WHITE
- ▼ GREY
- ⬤ BLACK

CHICKS
10 sts x 14 rows
Background colour is ecru.

CAT
10 sts x 14 rows
Background colour is pastel pink.

MOUSE
10 sts x 14 rows
Background colour is blue.

GOOSE
24 sts x 38 rows
Background colour is light blue.

JUMPING CAT
24 sts x 38 rows
Background colour is pastel blue.

SHEEPDOG
24 sts x 38 rows
Background colour is bright green.

COW
24 sts x 38 rows
Background colour is deep orange.

SHEEP
24 sts x 38 rows
Background colour is pastel pink.

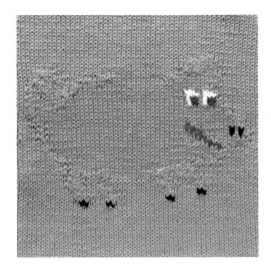

PIG
50 sts x 70 rows
Background
colour is
bright green.

**DUCK LAYING
EGGS**
50 sts x 70 rows
Background
colour is
aquamarine.

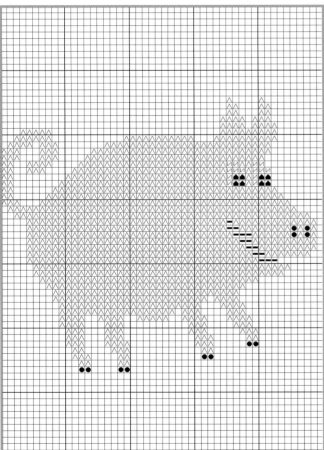

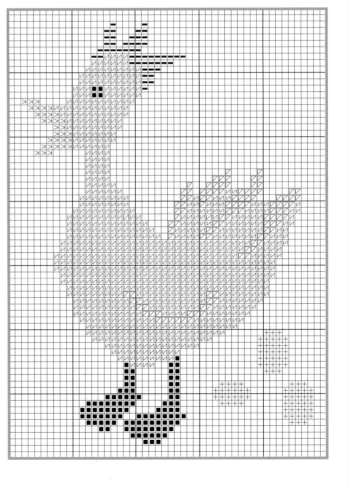

LIGHT KHAKI	
MID GREEN	
AQUAMARINE	
LIGHT BLUE	
PASTEL BLUE	
PALE GREY	
BLUE	
NAVY BLUE	
PURPLE	
DEEP PINK	
MID PINK	
PASTEL PINK	
RED	
DEEP ORANGE	
BRIGHT YELLOW	
MUSTARD	
BRIGHT GREEN	
OLD GOLD	
LIGHT BROWN	
BEIGE	
PALE YELLOW	
ECRU	
WHITE	
GREY	
BLACK	

A trip to the countryside

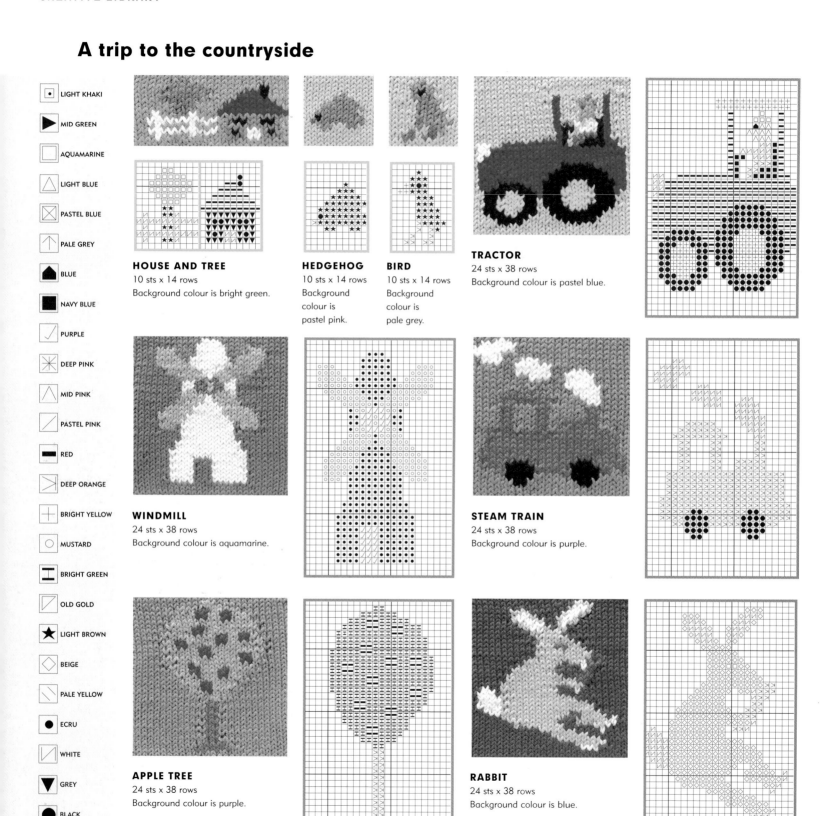

LIGHT KHAKI

MID GREEN

AQUAMARINE

LIGHT BLUE

PASTEL BLUE

PALE GREY

BLUE

NAVY BLUE

PURPLE

DEEP PINK

MID PINK

PASTEL PINK

RED

DEEP ORANGE

BRIGHT YELLOW

MUSTARD

BRIGHT GREEN

OLD GOLD

LIGHT BROWN

BEIGE

PALE YELLOW

ECRU

WHITE

GREY

BLACK

HOUSE AND TREE
10 sts x 14 rows
Background colour is bright green.

HEDGEHOG
10 sts x 14 rows
Background colour is pastel pink.

BIRD
10 sts x 14 rows
Background colour is pale grey.

TRACTOR
24 sts x 38 rows
Background colour is pastel blue.

WINDMILL
24 sts x 38 rows
Background colour is aquamarine.

STEAM TRAIN
24 sts x 38 rows
Background colour is purple.

APPLE TREE
24 sts x 38 rows
Background colour is purple.

RABBIT
24 sts x 38 rows
Background colour is blue.

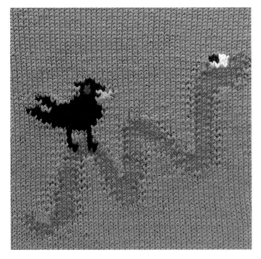

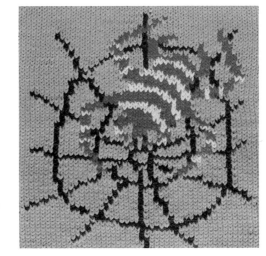

WORM AND BLACKBIRD
50 sts x 70 rows
Background colour is aquamarine.

SPIDER IN HIS WEB
50 sts x 70 rows
Background colour is purple.

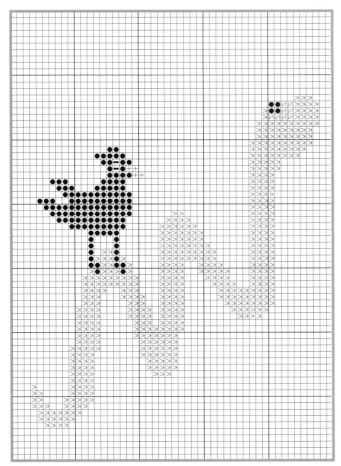

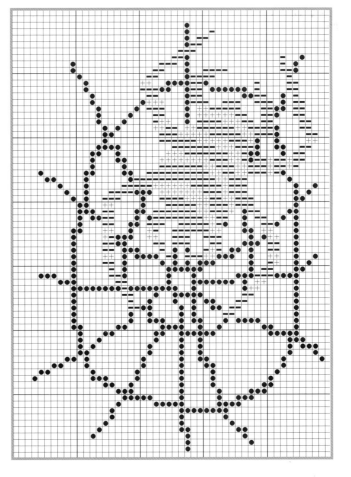

LIGHT KHAKI	
MID GREEN	
AQUAMARINE	
LIGHT BLUE	
PASTEL BLUE	
PALE GREY	
BLUE	
NAVY BLUE	
PURPLE	
DEEP PINK	
MID PINK	
PASTEL PINK	
RED	
DEEP ORANGE	
BRIGHT YELLOW	
MUSTARD	
BRIGHT GREEN	
OLD GOLD	
LIGHT BROWN	
BEIGE	
PALE YELLOW	
ECRU	
WHITE	
GREY	
BLACK	

Insects and flowers

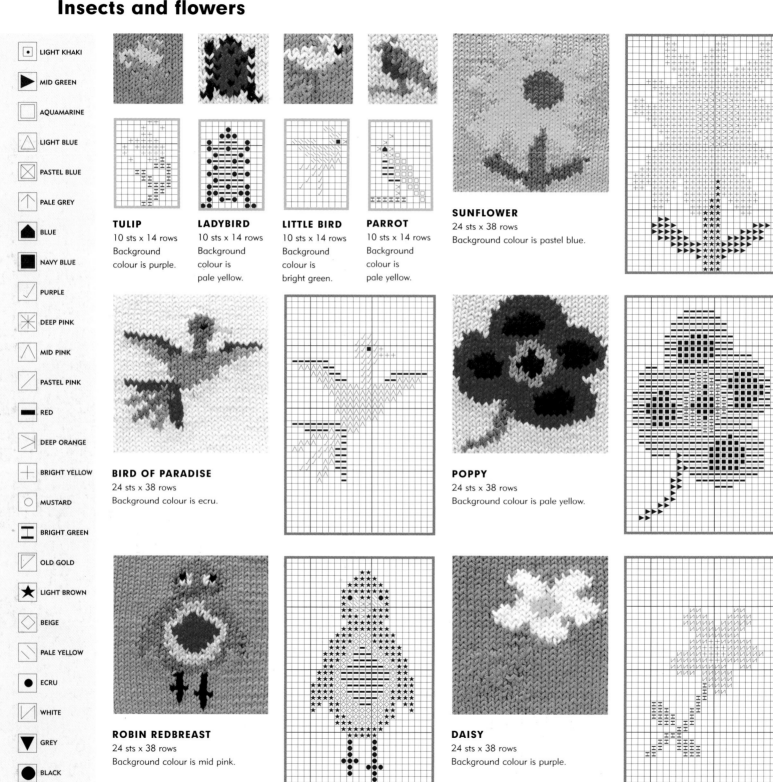

Key (symbols):

- ⊡ LIGHT KHAKI
- ▶ MID GREEN
- ▢ AQUAMARINE
- △ LIGHT BLUE
- ⊠ PASTEL BLUE
- ↑ PALE GREY
- ◆ BLUE
- ■ NAVY BLUE
- / PURPLE
- ✳ DEEP PINK
- △ MID PINK
- ◿ PASTEL PINK
- ▬ RED
- ◤ DEEP ORANGE
- + BRIGHT YELLOW
- ◯ MUSTARD
- ⊟ BRIGHT GREEN
- ◹ OLD GOLD
- ★ LIGHT BROWN
- ◇ BEIGE
- ◺ PALE YELLOW
- ● ECRU
- ◹ WHITE
- ▼ GREY
- ⬤ BLACK

TULIP
10 sts x 14 rows
Background colour is purple.

LADYBIRD
10 sts x 14 rows
Background colour is pale yellow.

LITTLE BIRD
10 sts x 14 rows
Background colour is bright green.

PARROT
10 sts x 14 rows
Background colour is pale yellow.

SUNFLOWER
24 sts x 38 rows
Background colour is pastel blue.

BIRD OF PARADISE
24 sts x 38 rows
Background colour is ecru.

POPPY
24 sts x 38 rows
Background colour is pale yellow.

ROBIN REDBREAST
24 sts x 38 rows
Background colour is mid pink.

DAISY
24 sts x 38 rows
Background colour is purple.

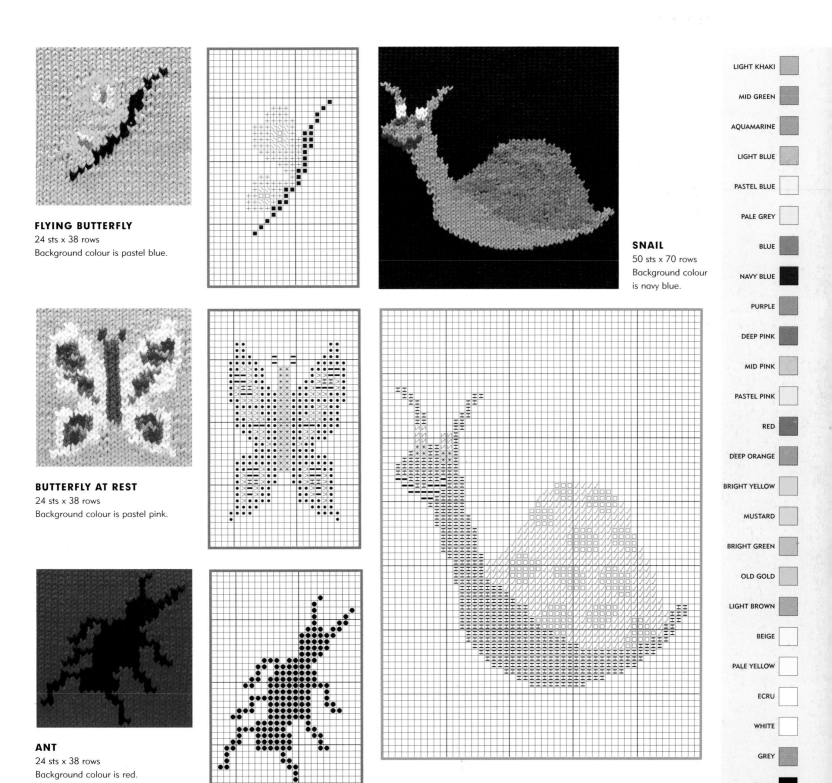

FLYING BUTTERFLY
24 sts x 38 rows
Background colour is pastel blue.

BUTTERFLY AT REST
24 sts x 38 rows
Background colour is pastel pink.

ANT
24 sts x 38 rows
Background colour is red.

SNAIL
50 sts x 70 rows
Background colour
is navy blue.

LIGHT KHAKI
MID GREEN
AQUAMARINE
LIGHT BLUE
PASTEL BLUE
PALE GREY
BLUE
NAVY BLUE
PURPLE
DEEP PINK
MID PINK
PASTEL PINK
RED
DEEP ORANGE
BRIGHT YELLOW
MUSTARD
BRIGHT GREEN
OLD GOLD
LIGHT BROWN
BEIGE
PALE YELLOW
ECRU
WHITE
GREY
BLACK

Insect and flowers

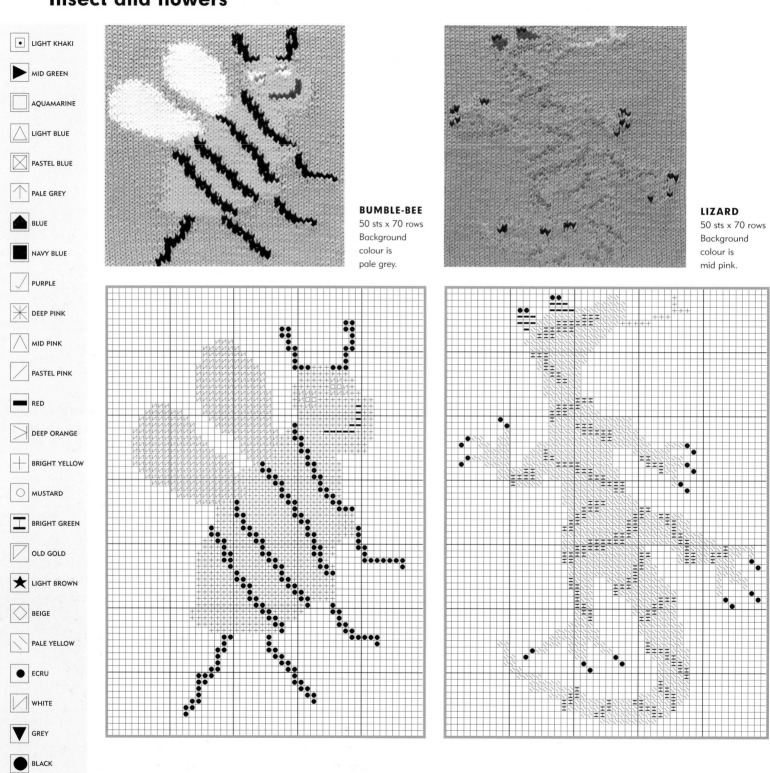

⊡	LIGHT KHAKI
▶	MID GREEN
▭	AQUAMARINE
△	LIGHT BLUE
⊠	PASTEL BLUE
↑	PALE GREY
⬟	BLUE
■	NAVY BLUE
✓	PURPLE
✳	DEEP PINK
∧	MID PINK
╱	PASTEL PINK
▬	RED
▷	DEEP ORANGE
+	BRIGHT YELLOW
○	MUSTARD
⊥	BRIGHT GREEN
╱	OLD GOLD
★	LIGHT BROWN
◇	BEIGE
╱	PALE YELLOW
●	ECRU
╱	WHITE
▼	GREY
⬤	BLACK

BUMBLE-BEE
50 sts x 70 rows
Background
colour is
pale grey.

LIZARD
50 sts x 70 rows
Background
colour is
mid pink.

122

Useful Techniques and Information

Mastering techniques

Casting on methods

THUMB METHOD

This produces an elastic edge and is suitable for garter and moss (seed) stitch. Use it when casting on for a collar, pocket or separate edging.

Make a slip knot, leaving a long tail, and place the loop on a needle. Holding the needle and the ball end of the yarn in your right hand, wrap the cut end of the yarn around your left thumb, from back to front. Insert the needle into this loop. Then bring the right-hand yarn

forward and over the needle, as shown. Draw the needle, with the newly formed loop, up through the loop on your thumb. Take your thumb out of the loop and pull the yarn tight on the needle with your left hand to complete the new stitch.

CABLE METHOD

This method produces a firm, hard-wearing edge, especially suitable for ribbing. It is worked using two needles.

Place a slip knot on the left needle. Insert the right needle into the loop. Holding the ball end of the yarn in your right hand, bring the yarn around the right needle from back to front, then pull it back between the two needle points. Draw the right needle back, pulling the yarn through the slip knot on the left needle, as shown. Then insert

the left needle through the loop, from right to left, and withdraw the right needle. You now have two stitches on the left needle. Insert the right needle between these two stitches, and make a new stitch as before, pulling it through the first two stitches, then transferring it to the left needle.

Intarsia

Intarsia is a method of knitting using separate balls, or bobbins, of yarn for each block of colour. The secret of intarsia knitting lies in the careful preparation.

Organize yourself before you start knitting, and prepare your yarns carefully in order to avoid any tangles.

When using bobbins, keep the unwound yarn as short as possible to prevent tangling.

To calculate the amount of yarn needed for small areas, wind the yarn around the needle the same number of times as the number of stitches in that area, then add a little extra yarn for securing the ends.

JOINING A NEW COLOUR

Insert the right needle into the next stitch. Bring the new (pink) yarn between the needle tips and across the old (blue) yarn [from left to right]. Take the new yarn under the old yarn, as shown, and knit the next stitch with it. Move the tail of the new yarn off the right needle as the new stitch is formed.

CHANGING COLOURS

On a knit row: Insert the right needle into the next stitch and place the old (blue) yarn over the new (pink) yarn, as shown above. Pull the new yarn up and knit the stitch.

On a purl row: Insert the right needle into the next stitch and place the old (blue) yarn over the new (pink) yarn. Pull the new yarn up and purl the stitch.

CARRYING YARN

To the right: On a knit row: insert the right needle into the next stitch. Take the carried (pink) yarn across the back of the work to the right, behind the old (blue) yarn. Knit the stitch.

To the left: On a knit row: insert the right needle into the next stitch. Take the carried (pink) yarn across the back of the work to left and across the other (blue) yarn. Knit the stitch. A loop is produced when moving a colour over more than three stitches. Catch this loop in as you go as follows.

On right side of work: On a knit row: insert the right needle into the next stitch, cross the carried (blue) yarn under the other (pink) yarn and knit the specified number of stitches with the carried (blue) yarn. To catch in the (blue) loop produced at the back of the work, insert the right needle into the next stitch and then down to pick up the loop. Knit the stitch, at the same time losing the loop.

On wrong side of work: On a purl row: insert the right needle into the next stitch, cross the carried (blue) yarn under the other (pink) yarn and purl the specified number of stitches with the carried (blue) yarn. To catch in the (blue) loop produced at the back of work, insert the right needle into the next stitch and then down to pick up the loop. Purl the stitch, at the same time losing the loop.

Short-row shaping

This method of shaping prevents a stepped effect on shoulder edges – for example, when a group of stitches are cast off, and instead produces a continuous sloped edge. One of the problems of short-row shaping is that wrapping the slipped stitch creates a visible loop around the stitch. However this loop can be hidden on the last row.

On a knit row: Work to point where knitting is to be turned. With yarn at back of work, slip the first stitch purlwise from left to right needle. Take yarn to front of work between needles and slip the stitch back onto left needle, then take yarn to back between needles. You have now wrapped the slipped stitch. Turn work.

To stop the loop around the slipped-stitch from showing, hide it on the last row as follows.

Pick up loop from the front with right needle. Lose loop by knitting it together with next stitch on the left needle.

On a purl row: Work to the point where knitting is to be turned. With yarn at front of work, slip first stitch purlwise from left to right needle. Take yarn to back of work between needles. Slip stitch back onto left needle, return yarn to front between needles. You have now wrapped the slipped stitch. Turn work.

To stop the slipped-stitch loop from showing, hide the loop on the last row as follows.

Pick up horizontal loop from behind with right needle. Lose loop by purling it together with next stitch on left needle.

Casting (binding) off two edges together

This is an ideal way of joining shoulder edges that are not shaped or those that have been shaped using the turning method of short-row shaping.

Hold the needles together in your left hand, with right sides of work facing each other and the

points of needles in same direction. Holding a third needle in your right hand, insert its point through the fronts of both stitches. Knit the first two stitches together. Repeat this process with the next pair of stitches. Using the tip of one of the left needles, pass the first stitch over the second stitch on the right needle. Drop stitch off needle. Continue in this way to produce a neat, seamless join.

Blocking and pressing

Before sewing up your garment, block each piece of knitting on a flat surface and (if the pattern so instructs) press it. This will ensure that all of the pieces are the correct shape and measurement. It will also prevent the edges of the pieces from curling, so that they are easier to sew together, and will give you a professional-looking garment.

Pin out each piece of knitting onto a padded board, checking as you go that the measurements match those in the instructions. Ease in or stretch out the pieces to remedy small discrepancies. For a flat fabric, place a damp cloth over the knitting and press the iron on the cloth; for a textured fabric, hold a steam iron just above it. Allow the pieces to dry before unpinning.

Sewing up

Secure all loose ends. Avoid using yarn ends from the knitting for sewing up as you may cut the main knitting if you have to undo them. Use a tapestry, or other blunt-pointed needle and a matching yarn for sewing up.

MATTRESS STITCH SEAM

This creates an invisible seam and is easy to work.

Place the two pieces to be joined right side up and side by side on a flat surface. Insert the needle between the first and second stitches on the first row of the edge.

Take the needle under the next row and pull the yarn through, leaving a long end. Repeat this in the opposite edge, but this time bring the needle out two rows above the starting point. Insert the needle into the first edge again, into the place where the yarn emerges. Bring it out two rows above that point.

Repeat, zigzagging from edge to edge, for about 5cm (2in), then pull the thread tight to create an invisible seam. Continue in this way to the end. Darn in the yarn ends securely.

Joining ribbed fabrics: When joining ribbed edges, work half a stitch instead of a full stitch in

from the edge. This allows a complete stitch to be formed from the two halves.

Joining stitches to rows: When sewing in sleeves start at the centre point of both edges, inserting the needle and yarn at this point in the usual way. Pin the edges together to ensure that the seams are joined evenly. Starting at the centre point, work mattress stitch along each side in turn.

FLAT SEAM

This is used for sewing on button bands, edgings and collars. Use it also for joining ribbed sections of garments such as cuffs, where a neat, flat seam is essential.

Place the two pieces right sides together, and hold the edges between the index finger and thumb of the left hand. From the back of the work, insert the needle through the back of the knot of the edge stitches and pull yarn through both pieces. Continue sewing in this way, working a stitch on every second row.

Abbreviations

alt	alternate	**P**	purl	
beg	beginning/begin	**P1b**	purl next *st* through	
C2B	place the next *st* on		the back loop	
	cn, leave at back of	**P2tog**	purl next 2 *sts* together	
	work, K1, K1 from *cn*	**P2togb**	purl next 2 *sts* together	
C3B	place the next 2 *sts* on		through the back loops	
	cn, leave at back of	**patt**	pattern	
	work, K1, K2 from *cn*	**rem**	remain(ing)	
C3F	place the next *st* on	**rep**	repeat	
	cn, leave at front of	**rev st st**	reverse stocking	
	work, K2, K1 from *cn*		(stockinette) stitch	
C4B	place the next 2 *sts* on	**RS**	right side	
	cn, leave at back of	**sl**	slip next *st*	
	work, K2, K2 from *cn*	**sl2(3)**	slip next 2(3) *sts*	
C4F	place the next 2 *sts* on	**sl1 K1 psso**	slip 1 *st*, knit 1 *st*, pass	
	cn, leave at front of		slipped *st* over	
	work, K2, K2 from *cn*	**st(s)**	stitch(es)	
cm	centimetre	**st st**	stocking (stockinette)	
cn	cable needle		stitch	
cont	continue	**T2B**	place the next *st* on	
DK	double knitting		*cn*, leave at back of	
dec	decreas(e)(ing)		work, K1, P1 from *cn*	
foll	follow(s)(ing)	**T2F**	place the next *st* on	
inc	increas(e)(ing)		*cn*, leave at front of	
in(s)	inch(es)		work, P1, K1 from *cn*	
K	knit	**T3B**	place the next *st* on	
K1b	knit next *st* through		*cn*, leave at back of	
	the back loop		work, K2, P1 from *cn*	
K2tog	knit next 2 *sts*	**T3F**	place the next 2 *sts* on	
	together		*cn*, leave at front of	
K2togb	knit next 2 *sts*		work, P1, K2 from *cn*	
	together through the	**tog**	together	
	back loops	**WS**	wrong side	
K3tog	knit next 3 *sts*	**yb**	yarn to back of work	
	together	**yf**	yarn to front of work	
K3togb	knit next 3 *sts*	**yfwd**	yarn forward	
	together through the	**yo**	yarn over needle	
	back loops	**▶ or ▶▶**	repeat instructions	
MB	make a bobble		between ▶ or ▶▶ as	
mm	millimetre		many times as	
oz	ounce(s)		instructed	

Substituting yarns

Knitting patterns always specify a particular brand of yarn. Throughout this book we have used Rowan Handknit DK Cotton, which is a medium-weight cotton yarn (100% cotton) with approximately 85m (92yd) per 50g (1¾oz) ball. If you need to purchase a substitute yarn be sure to calculate the number of balls or hanks by the metre (yard) rather than by yarn weight.

Yarn colour

Throughout the book we have used generic colour names. If you choose to use a different yarn to the one suggested then match the shade as closely as possible or choose a different colour if you prefer. See below for the equivalent Rowan Handknit DK Cotton shade for the generic colour:

Generic colour	Rowan colour name
light khaki	Foggy
mid green	Soft Green
aquamarine	Oasis
light blue	Ice Water
pastel blue	Raindrop
pale grey	Chime
blue	Diana
navy blue	Turkish Plum
purple	Gerba
deep pink	Carmen
mid pink	Sugar
pastel pink	Fruit Salad
red	Rosso
deep orange	Flame
bright yellow	Sunflower
mustard	Popcorn
bright green	Gooseberry
old gold	Artichoke
light brown	Tope
beige	Linen
pale yellow	Zing
ecru	Ecru
white	Bleached
grey	Muddy
black	Black

> **CONVERTING WEIGHTS AND LENGTHS**
>
> oz = g x 0.0352
> g = oz x 28.35
> in = cm x 0.3937
> cm = in x 2.54
> yd = m x 0.9144
> m = yd x 1.0936

Index

Suppliers

Rowan Yarns are widely available. For a stockist near you or mail-order details, telephone Rowan Yarns direct on 01484 681 881 or visit their website on www.knitrowan.com.

For more information on suppliers outside the UK, contact the Rowan distributor listed for your country below:

BELGIUM: Pavan, Koningin Astridlaan 78, B9000 Gent.
  Tel: (32) 9 221 8591
CANADA: Diamond Yarn, 9697 St Laurent, Montreal, Quebec, H3L 2N1. Tel: (514) 388 6188
  Diamond Yarn (Toronto), 155 Martin Ross, Unit 3, Toronto, Ontario, M3J 2L9. Tel: (416) 736 6111
FRANCE: Elle Tricot, 8 Rue du Coq, 67000 Strasbourg.
  Tel: (33) 3 88 23 03 13

GERMANY: Wolle & Design, Wolfshovener Strasse 76, 52428 Julich-Stetternich. Tel: (49) 2461 54735
HOLLAND: de Afstap, Oude Leliestraat 12, 1015 AW Amsterdam.
  Tel: (31) 20 6231445
HONG KONG: East Unity Co. Ltd, Unit B2, 7/F, Block B, Kailey Industrial Centre, 12 Fung Yip Street, Chai Wan.
  Tel: (852) 2869 7110
ICELAND: Storkurinn, Kjorgardi, Laugavegi 59, Reykjavik.
  Tel: (354) 551 82 58
JAPAN: DiaKeito Co. Ltd, 2-3-11 Senba-Higashi, Minoh City, Osaka. Tel: (81) 727 27 6604
SWEDEN: Wincent, Norrtulsgaten 65, 11345 Stockholm.
  Tel: (46) 8 673 70 60
U.S.A.: Rowan USA, 5 Northern Boulevard, Amherst, New Hampshire 03031. Tel: (1 603) 886 5041/5043

8/03